unWorthy

A STORY OF REDEMPTION AND HOPE

unWorthy

CLAUDIA RAMOS

Foreword by Michelle Matoga

CAYA'S
BOOKS

unWorthy

© 2023 by CLAUDIA RAMOS

Typeset by Michelle Cline

All rights reserved solely by the author. The author guarantees
all contents are original and do not infringe upon the legal rights
of any other person or work. No part of this book may be repro-
duced in any form without the permission of the author. The views
expressed in this book are not necessarily those of the publisher.

All Scripture quotations are from The Passion Translation®.
Copyright © 2017, 2018, 2020 by Passion & Fire
Ministries, Inc. Used by permission. All rights reserved.
ThePassionTranslation.com.

Printed in the United States of America.
ISBN: 979-8-218-00859-8
LCCN: 2022909647

Caya's Books
Revere, Massachusetts

TABLE OF CONTENTS

ACKNOWLEDGMENT

The story that follows is my story of redemption and hope. Redemption because I've been redeemed by my savior. Hope because it will give you, the reader, hope that if I've been redeemed so can you. I am not a victim; I am a child of the Most High God. As a consequence of childhood abuse by my earthly father and other men, I lived a life full of mistakes and bad choices.

Penning my memoir was difficult and though this book was a project that was supposed to be completed in six months, it took over a year. There were many times that I questioned whether or not I should expose myself in this way. By exposing myself, I would also expose those who caused me pain, but mostly because I kept many of my secrets hidden from my girls. Being a mom is the most rewarding gift and best job of my life. The thought of hurting my children is something I almost can't bear. However, I hope that others can find healing through my pain and understand that you can overcome anything. I worked with wonderful people who helped guide me through this process. Martha, thank you from the bottom of my heart for helping me put this together and for praying with me. You are a resilient woman, and your story should also be told. Peter, thanks for believing in this project and giving me the chance to tell my story.

To my Lord, thank You for chasing me until I could not escape!

Thank You for saving me and dying for me.

I must thank my husband, my rock, my best friend and the cheerleader in my corner, Dave. Babe, you mean so much to me and though you may not be my first love, you are my last. I have never loved anyone the way I love you. You showed me what a healthy marriage looks like. I am forever grateful to God for putting you in my path to use us both for His glory! You make me smile and love my life.

To my daughters, (now, I am totally emotional) I love you with a love that cannot be explained. It is a love that comes from the deepest part of my heart and my soul. If I did not do anything right in my life, I know that I did the best I could as your mom and I love you more and more each day. You kept me alive when I wanted to die. You are my world!

To my twin and childhood best friend, I thank God for you because, unbeknownst to you, you kept me going. I love and admire you so much. You are the best sister in the entire universe. I could not have lived the hell I lived and survived all those years if I didn't have you in my life and by my side.

Para mi madre, mami la amo con todo mi corazón. No tengo palabras para agradecerle su sacrificio. Eres la mejor madre del mundo. Una bendicion de Dios.

To my pastors, Zenzo & Michelle, you are the epitome of Christ's love! I cannot thank you enough for allowing me to serve under your leadership. I love you so much and I thank God for you!

To the rest of my family, thank you for putting up with me. I am so far from being perfect but you accept me the way I am.

To every single man that hurt me, I forgive you and I love you with the love of Christ, despite the hurt. To every person I've hurt and caused pain, please forgive me. I was lost in a world I did not belong in.

To the reader, I do not know you but I love you and I pray that you are blessed by my story.

If you are in a situation where you are being abused, please find someone to talk to and share what you are going through. Reach out to the National Domestic Violence Hotline at www.thehotline.org or in the US 1.800.799.SAFE. YOU ARE NOT ALONE!

FOREWORD

Are you in need of rescuing? Does your heart ache for another's life to be restored? Do you need to find hope in a circumstance that seems hopeless?

This is one woman's powerful story of hope and redemption. Claudia beautifully, vulnerably and open-heartedly shares her story—a life that took her through unthinkable abuse resulting in a loss of her desire to live. Shaken to the core and questioning this life as she knew it, Claudia shares how God rescued her and turned the turmoil into a testimony.

If you have ever doubted God; if you are at a place of apathy in your life; if you ever wondered if your situation is too hard for Him, you will want to read this book. I am excited for the pages that are to follow and the newfound hope you are to discover through them as you read through unWorthy.

The God of all creation, the God of the universe chose to give up His life for us, to rescue us. He redeemed us. His beautiful redemption power is shown over and over again throughout our lives as He reveals Himself throughout our life's circumstances. His power is shown through the life of Claudia Ramos.

I have had the privilege of being Claudia's pastor for the past few years and I have yet to meet a more loving, resilient, forgiving, kind- hearted soul as hers. These pages speak of the beautiful, transformed life she is now living. All glory to God. Though the trials and the anguish and pain sought to break and trap her in a life of misery, she chose to follow God's voice and allow Him in her life. And today, she is living a life of freedom. Her scars no longer bind her with reminders of pain, but are a continual reminder of God's redemptive power and love.

Whether you're in the darkest place of your life right now, experienced similar hurts and pains, or you are grasping for a deeper compassion and understanding of the people that surround you every day, this book will prove to be a comfort, encouragement and inspiration.

Nothing is impossible for Him. He cares for you just as He cares for Claudia. He will do it for you just as He did it for her. Don't wait another moment! Read on to begin your own redemptive story. You'll never be the same again!

-Pastor Michelle Matoga Impact Church, MA

INTRODUCTION

Growing up, I had a memorable life. Just like any young girl, I had beautiful moments with my family. I also experienced many moments that were terrifying. Moments that no girl should ever have to endure. However, even in the midst of all of that, God looked out for me and blessed me with a great life companion, the best friend any girl could have. Although at the time I was unaware of Psalm 139 which states, "that He knew me in my mother's womb," I understand now that GOD knew my journey enough to bless me with such a friend. My best friend had my back even before we knew what that meant. I always knew I could count on her and she always knew she could count on me too. We didn't have to say a word; we could communicate without speaking. You could say that we read each other's thoughts and were there for one another 24/7. She was a distraction from many painful moments; she was my cheerleader during times of joy. My partner in crime and my confidant – the one God chose to share my mother's womb – my twin!

As a child, I would often lay awake at night. Staring at the sky, I imagined building a ladder long enough to reach the clouds. Even as achild, I found peace in the sky. It is hard to explain, but I imagined that everything I wanted could be found in the sky. Peace, memories and my mom were all waiting for me if I could just build that ladder. You see, when I was a child my life was hard. My dad was abusive, my family was poor and my mom left us. She wasn't a bad mom or bad person, quite the opposite, she was and still is an amazing woman. I can still remember it like it was yesterday. A strong, resilient woman, my mom, made the choice to leave us behind so that she could save us. My family all watched as mom's plane took off and faded into the distance. Perhaps, that is why I continued to look for her in the sky, behind the clouds. As a child, I simply thought it was a gesture, an attempt to remember my mom. As I grew older, I realized it was more than that. It was an attempt to find something greater, or someone greater. Now I see I was like the psalmist in Psalm 121:1. Just as he looked to the hills for help, I looked to the clouds. I remembered what my mom was like before she left and prayed for the day that she would return. This is my story.

LOOKING UP To THE SKY: WHERE MY HOPE COMES FROM

Chapter One
THE EARLY YEARS

My early years started out quite ordinary – a typical family in Colombia. Pereira, the city where I was born, is a beautiful and busy place and you can see mountains from almost anywhere. Although not an affluent city, everyone lives happily and loves to play music, dance, and smile. It is also known as the Eje Cafetero (Coffee Axis) or the coffee capital. My family didn't lack for much – my dad owned a grocery store with a butcher shop. My parents had a beautiful house built with enough room for the five of us (mom, dad and three girls). We had two new cars and most of the accommodations that a family could ever need. The view from the outside seemed like the ideal family. However, on the inside another story was unfolding. We watched our drunken father verbally and physically abuse our mother. We witnessed the behavior of a woman walking on eggshells, afraid to disrupt the flow of her husband in fear of setting him off. It was a life of terror in a war that she did not deserve.

We witnessed the behavior of a man who was unfaithful to his wife with various women, yet he promised that he loved her the most. Despite the abuse, that possibly began as just mere ugly words but eventually progressed into physical abuse, my mom stayed. Perhaps, she felt like any other woman stuck in a similar situation. She had three little girls who needed her. My mom would care for us as best as she could. She took on the responsibility of keeping our family together, despite the many nights she was left alone. Every morning, mom would wake up early and fix breakfast for our dad before he headed out to the wholesaler to pick up the meat for our butcher shop. Eventually, his personal excursions became so frequent that he was out almost every night. To ease his burden and be more of a contributor, my mom would even go to help him out at the store.

Finally, he reached a point where his morning trips to the wholesaler became less. One day, when mom woke him up, he begrudgingly confessed that he had run out of money and could not afford to buy anything else at the wholesaler. Soon after, he came home with news that he was selling the family business. The loss was even greater for my mom. Now that he had more time on his hands, he increased the level of abuse toward her. She could not do anything right in his eyes! There were times we witnessed our dad chase our mom with a knife because she said "the wrong thing" or "used the wrong tone." Once, he exploded just because she made a comment about a song he was playing over and over. Mom had to tread carefully around this man, and always be mindful of what she would say.

There were instances when my mom would escape my dad's wrath and run to her parent's house, my abuelos. But, whenever she felt that false sense of "security" she came back to the abusive home. Ironically, once she arrived, he wouldn't allow her inside the house. We had no choice but to pry open a window for our mom so she could enter.

Before long, my dad grew tired of staying home and found work as a salesman. This job meant he was away for days at a time selling shoes in the surrounding cities. His time away from home gave my mom several days of peace and safety. However, it was short-lived. Every time my dad returned, he would interrogate my mom on what she had been doing. This is typical in abusive scenarios – I now understand the reasons my mom feared full disclosure.

On one occasion while my dad was traveling, mom decided to go out with a couple of her friends for a night of dancing. It wasn't long before she returned home because she could not enjoy herself. Mom was always apprehensive about having fun. Upon his return, the questions began. Initially, my mom subtly mentioned a birthday party at a neighbor's home. She chose to withhold the details due to the panic and fear of possibly being physically abused. My dad saw right through the lie. Walking away from my mom, he threatened to call the neighbors to corroborate the story unless she told the truth. Realizing this, my mom almost immediately confessed. In a rage, he chased her across the house to beat her. Luckily, she was able to run to a neighbor's home to "wait out" his fury as one weathers a storm. She would always gauge when it was ok to return home.

At one point, my mom got a job. She wanted to help out with the household expenses, but it also served as an opportunity for her to get away from my dad as well. In order to work, she had to hire a babysitter, but this woman was mean to us. Of course, she never did anything in front of our mom, but when mom realized our negative change in behavior was due to this woman she fired the sitter and returned home full-time.

One day, while at the dining table, my dad nonchalantly made another announcement. Similar to when he sold the business, unbeknown to my mom, he sold our home. My mom was visibly shocked. There was no reason for us to have to sell our house. Wanting to ask questions, she refrained. Whatever his reasoning, it wasn't worth the argument that would follow for questioning his decision. The irony of the matter was that my dad had not given a single thought to where we would live. That crucial decision he left to my mom. Using her resourcefulness, she was able to fix his ill-planned mess and found us a place to live.

As I recall, our new house wasn't anything special, but it was a home. We moved into a neighborhood that seemed like a gypsy community. Since we moved quite often, we didn't make many friends. We all began to accept the family environment. An environment of instability and my dad's cruelty. He was such an unhappy and savage man that his brutality extended to everything around him- even our pets. One day my sister's dog was crying, I don't remember exactly why, but the poor animal wanted attention. Rather than take it outside or feed it, my dad locked the puppy in a drawer to drown out the noise. It was during this time that we all began to withdraw and walk on eggshells. My mom was the only constant person in our lives.

Still not learning his lesson, my dad continued to make decisions on his own that affected our family. Since selling our home and quitting his job as a shoe salesman, he was working as a bus driver. I guess he assumed he didn't need our second car since he now had free transportation, so he sold that vehicle. This would've been fine, but he also lent our remaining vehicle to a friend. As luck would have it, the friend totaled the car in an accident and we were left with no transportation other than the bus. Due to fear of speaking up, mom remained silent again.

Time passed on, we were getting used to our new reality when my dad brought home the biggest surprise – a strange and permanent surprise. One afternoon, my dad came home for lunch accompanied by a young boy. Despite this toddler's dirty appearance, he was rather handsome. My mom asked what was going on. My dad explained that during his bus route a woman tried to kill this little boy. Apparently, my dad saw her trying to throw this child into oncoming traffic. Portraying himself as a saint, my dad told everyone he just happened to be in the right place at the right time to save this boy's life. What didn't make sense was why he brought the boy home. Rather than taking him to the police station or the church, he chose to bring Carlos Andres home. Of course, we had many questions–who even does something like this? My dad's story seemed to have many loose ends, but mom knew better than to question him. Mom immediately fell in love with my new brother and tenderly washed him clean. As for me, I was thrilled to have a new playmate and someone to run around with.

Following this incident, we tried to resume to some normalcy. My dad continued his routine. Leaving early in the morning to drive his bus route and returning late in the evening. That is if he returned at all. He still found a way to disappear on mom. One day, my dad's bus was reported stolen. He had parked it in front of the house as he had always done. Later that week, the bus was found torched in a nearby neighborhood. A few nights later, I was awakened as my parents were talking about the incident. A police officer took my dad into custody while they continued to investigate the robbery and destruction of the bus.

Meanwhile, my siblings and I went to spend time with my grandparents (from my dad's side) in Cali, a city just a couple hours away from our home. Upon his release from jail, he gathered some of his belongings and left to see a woman who also lived in Cali. My mom, in a state of confusion, decided to stay with her folks for a few days. During the entire time, dad never called my mom to check on her. The only time mom heard from him was to ask if she was going to pick us up at his parents' home. It was not a question in my mom's heart. Of course, she was coming for us!

What a joyous day when mom arrived with my abuela (her mom) to pick us up. I had missed my mom so much. I missed her kisses, her smile and her warm hugs! I missed her so much because in my eyes, she was the coolest, most precious woman in the world. However, that joy was short lived because my father emotionally tortured her by refusing to let us go home with her. Mom pleaded relentlessly with him, but he refused. Fighting back her tears, with her voice shaking, my mom responded, "the only way I would leave my children with you is if they want to stay," my mom knew that we would not want to stay without her. My dad responded with a smug, arrogant smile, "agreed." Turning to us he asked, "Girls, do you want to stay with me or return with your mom?"

Without missing a beat, we told him we wanted to go home with mom! As if taken by surprise, he conceded; however, he did not allow my brother (the one he brought home that afternoon) to leave with mom. Devastated and realizing she had no say in the matter, she left my brother behind.

My poor mom left with tears in her eyes. If it were up to her, she would have also taken my brother home. She loved that boy as if he was her own since the moment he came through our door. That was the kind of man my dad was. He knew he could hurt my mom by holding Carlos Andres back, and somehow that gave him a sense of power and satisfaction. Nodding her head to consent and putting her pride aside, mom asked my dad if he would give her some money to buy food for the trip home. His response was so callused and cruel, "the only thing I would give you is poison."

That day my dad stayed in Cali to be with his mistress and never showed remorse for leaving his wife and small girls. He never returned home.

Chapter Two

MOMENTARY BLISS

*"Though we experience every kind of pressure,
we're not crushed. At times we don't know what to do,
but quitting is not an option"*
2 Corinthians 4:8

Freed from an abusive relationship and determined to pave the way to a better life, my mom was a model of resilience and strength! In the interim, we moved in with her parents, my abuelos, while she studied a secretarial course, but ultimately she found a job at a pharmacy. There was nothing that was going to stand in my mom's way. She was determined to provide us a better life as a single mom. I can still close my eyes and remember the time she came into my room and kneeled by the bed with a bottle of hot chocolate. She kissed my forehead and went to work. I have so many vivid memories. I always thought she was so cool. I wanted to be just like her. I remember one night, as we were brushing our teeth before bedtime, a little bit of toothpaste dripped on the side of her mouth and I allowed the toothpaste to do the same, so I could be just like my mom.

My mom's love was always demonstrated in her tender care, warm-heartedness and joy when we were together. She was always so affectionate with her kisses and caresses.

There was never a doubt that she enjoyed motherhood. Her eyes always displayed the love of her choice to be a mom.

Mom hoped to give her daughters a better future and a happier life. In stark comparison to our dad, she was the embodiment of pure love. Now that she was in a better environment, an environment where she did not have to carefully consider her words and actions, she could be free and was able to show us even more of her true self. She loved us so much. Once, I caught her doing our laundry, and as she was folding the clothes, she would put them near her nose and breathe in deeply. Even our scent was special to her. Every morning, she would wake up before the sun and make us a warm breakfast before sending us on our way to school. There were so many memories from this time. I didn't know it then, but these memories would bring life to me in many lonely moments to come.

Our life was a dream. Unfortunately, just like any dream, you have to wake up. I remember the day clearly.

Even though everything seemed amazing with dad gone, my mom realized that she couldn't provide us with a stable future if things kept going the way they were. For the last year, she had worked and sacrificed so much to give us a good life, but it was barely enough. My mom made a tough decision. It was a Saturday morning and she called us all to the living room. My mom sat facing me and my two sisters with tears in her eyes. It was obvious that this was not an easy choice for her. She told us she was going on a long trip to visit my aunt in New York. Her plan was to work hard and save enough money so one day we could be together again. Clearly, she thought of the sacrifices and the high cost, but she was determined and knew that the reward would be a better future.

Her departure was memorable; it was quite a poignant goodbye – especially for a young child. My mom's departure date was scheduled for April 4th. My mom was leaving on my birthday! Oh, the sadness in those memories. I clearly remember the airport; I was kissing mom as her arms wrapped around us. The sorrow in her eyes was imprinted on my heart and my mind forever. Funny, on many occasions I used to look in her eyes to know whether things would be ok. That day I could not fully understand what was unfolding. All I remember is the pain we felt. My mom walked away but quickly turned around for one more look, she was brokenhearted! Once again, her eyes moved me to feel just as broken.

We watched the plane take off and saw it disappear into the cloudy sky. As silly as it sounds, this was when my dreams of building a ladder into the sky began. I imagined that if I could get to the clouds, I could find my mom.

This was a transformational moment that changed everything in our lives. Although a better future was on our horizon – it was still the most terrifying time. After all, my father was still the same monster!

Chapter Three

LIFE WITHOUT MOM

*"God, You're such a safe
and powerful place to find refuge!
You're a proven help in time of trouble—
more than enough and always available
whenever I need You"*
Psalm 46:1

We stayed under the care of my abuelos – my mom's parents. They did the best they could, but we were a handful. The years that followed were a delicate balance of bliss and pain.

I deeply missed my mom. Not a day went by that I didn't think about her. I missed everything about her. I had watched her many times inhale the scent of our clothes, so I found articles of hers and would place them close to my nose and breathe in. Even though they had been washed, in my mind there was the familiar scent of my mom that even the detergent could not erase.

Now that my mom was gone, my twin became my constant companion. She and I developed such a deep alliance that we became each other's defender. Back then, getting "out of line" meant you'd get a beating, no questions asked! That would occur quite often as we'd become troublemakers! You knew it was bad when my abuela, in her anger, would ask us to go get the "correa" which she used to punish us. This correa was not a belt, but a whip that originated from my Pucho's upholstery business. He upholstered buses and cars, so leather and vinyl materials were often found at home. My abuela would ask him to cut strips of these materials so she could whip us into shape. Sometimes, she soaked them in water and left them to dry in the sun. Once the leather dried, it would harden. I remember staring at it lying in the sun; as if it were waiting for me to get "out of line." Whenever we misbehaved, my abuela would have us go retrieve the whip and beat the mistake out of us. She hoped that we would learn our lesson, but we rarely did. Before you get too upset, you should know that I deserved most of the beatings that she gave me. I was always getting into some kind of trouble. The problem was the beatings would never change anything. I wasn't acting up because I wanted to be bad. It was my way of expressing anger and sadness. Poor abuelos, instead of enjoying their golden years they were caring for three not so easy-going girls. We had become disobedient and disrespectful; my mom's departure made us go rogue! The alliance between my twin and I was so close-knit that instead of "fessing up" when one of us misbehaved – we chose to be punished together. Truth is, if only one of us was punished, we both felt the wrath of the punishment. Perhaps that's why we hardly admitted to any specific incident – we both ended up in trouble and we wouldn't have had it any other way. There was nothing we wouldn't do for each other.

The notion that we had everything because we had each other became a reality. While living with my abuelos, we discovered we lived a bit different than when we were in our parent's home. We didn't have much, and we didn't live a life of luxury but that was okay. Living with our abuelos was the first time we had settled down long enough to set roots and make lots of friends! We were so lucky to find children our age with plenty of toys and a willingness to share. One

Christmas our friend received a pair of roller skates. We were just as happy as she was that you would have thought it was us who received them. It wasn't very practical but my twin and I preferred to play together with one skate each rather than just taking turns using the skates one at a time.

Despite not having much, my abuela made sure that our house was always in pristine condition. One of my favorite chores was cleaning the floor. It wasn't just mere mopping; it involved throwing down tons of water and soap. We would slide back and forth while scrubbing the floor and have so much fun doing it. My twin and I tried to make an adventure out of everyday chores. We would clean our furniture until not even a fingerprint could be seen. I felt a sense of pride at the end of my tasks. I had done a good job.

Many afternoons were spent in front of the TV watching shows with our abuelos. They were fans of Miami Vice, The Hulk and the A- Team. My abuelo, Pucho, was almost deaf so he would cup his hands around his ears to help him hear. When he turned on his old record player to play the tangos and boleros, you could literally hear the tunes almost at the other end of the street and we lived on the corner. Pucho was 100% the best grandpa in the entire universe. We would dance to his old records and sway from side to side. To this very day, I can close my eyes and go back to those afternoons. I can still smell the pipe my abuelo smoked for most of his life.

Despite our terrible behavior, life was great with my abuelos. Although mom left us, she certainly never forgot us and always provided. She had no advanced education, so she got a job as a factory worker making minimum wage. Mom sent envelopes with letters and money to my abuela to help with living expenses. I loved reading her notes and admired her handwriting. Especially the way she would write the C in my name, and before I knew it I started imitating it. I've met so many hardworking women – but they all pale in comparison to the immense challenges my mom endured. She often explained how she would budget her expenses to a minimum; she became savvy with her money and made smart purchases. The moment she could fill a box with items she would ship them to us. Usually, these would coincide with holidays or celebrations.

We looked forward to receiving those boxes; she would send the best clothes and a toy for us. I remember the feeling of wearing the shirt or pants that came straight from New York. I instantly felt so cool. It didn't even matter that the top and bottom did not match! Looking back, I'm not sure how she could even afford to live while sending us everything she did.

Another happy childhood memory was our ability to fundraise. We would cook red potatoes at home and make a guiso (a tomato and onion sauce). Then, we would go door to door selling them to help pay for a school trip or some other activity. My mom was already sending money for more important things. I think grandma decided it may be too much to ask my mom to send even more money. The truth is we didn't mind raising money for school. This meant we would be outside talking to our neighbors and seeing our friends. Life was great!

Memories of times spent in friends' homes during parties come back to me as I write. I learned to dance at a young age and would attend as many parties as my abuela would allow. Grandma was the authoritarian and grandpa was the "lenient" one and always looked out for us. Every time he went downtown, he would bring us a pastry when he returned home. He would also give us his change to go to the store and buy candy. I still miss him very much. These are a few of many happy childhood memories.

Shortly after my mom arrived in the U.S.A., my aunt had disappeared after dropping her daughter off at school. A couple of days later, her body was found in a dumpster in The Bronx. She was brutally murdered. How unfathomable, such a senseless act took my aunt's life. I cannot imagine the despair and deep pain my mom endured as she had to identify her sister's body at the morgue. My aunt was survived by her little girl who was just 5 years old. My mom suffered such misfortune shortly after arriving in the United States.

There were times that my twin and I would lay down on the floor and stare up at the sky. We constantly played "what does that cloud look like." Although I enjoyed looking at the shapes of the clouds, I'd mostly gaze at them to picture my mom up there – on those days she felt so far away. Looking at the clouds would bring me joy, peace and even hope that I would see my mom one day soon. I believe that God was providing me that peace that I could not get on my own.

Not too long after–my behavior began to get worse. I became more defiant and fighting became more frequent. I didn't back down from an argument. Instead of diffusing situations, I escalated them to the point that brawling was not a big deal. I was hurting inside and needed an outlet for my pain.

Chapter Four

MY FATHER'S WAYS

You will be guarded by God himself.
You will be safe when you leave your home,
and safely you will return.
He will protect you now,
and he'll protect you forevermore!
Psalm 121:8

Every year during vacation we would go visit my father in Cali; this is where he remained since he left my mom. Back then, the car ride was about six hours with no easy way to get there. These trips were horrible, and I dreaded almost everything about those visits. The only thing positive about them was being reunited with my little brother, Carlos Andres. My dad's abusive behavior worsened! He began sexually assaulting me.

I can't remember the first time it happened. As it is found in Psalm 86:15, I believe that because God is merciful and full of compassion, He erased from my recollection the first time the abuse began. I remember one night during one of our visits, I was in bed with my sister. My father came near and pulled me by the hand and took me to his bed. I closed my eyes so tightly as if doing this would make it not real. I felt the warmth of his breath on my skin and the smell of his cheap cologne clung onto my skin. I knew better than to make any noise or move. I would lie there screaming inside my head but would make no noise. I was as still as a statue. Lying there I would try to remove myself from the present and go somewhere pleasant in my mind, I would replay the day's events, or I would go back to earlier in the day when I was playing with my sister and brother or doing something fun. That became the pattern, the new normal—night after night, year after year. I hated when nighttime came because he would take out his frustrations on me and use me to fulfill his sick desires. Usually, he would not say a word; he would rape me and once he was done he would always say the same thing, "I do this because I love you, and as your dad, I can do this." He threatened me into keeping this secret by saying that he would find a way to kill my mom. It took me decades to understand that this is not the love of the Father. My earthly father was not my hiding place and couldn't protect me, even from himself.

During one of our visits, we went to his parents' house for a New Year's Eve party. After a night full of fun activities, I was so tired that I went to bed. The music coming from the other room was loud, but I was ready to go to sleep. As I laid in bed at his parents' house, I was grateful and relieved thinking I would not endure the sexual abuse tonight. No way would this happen tonight. There was a lot going on and everyone was having a good time. I slept through the noise of people laughing. I was startled awake by his words. He whispered, "come with me." Then, he took me to another room and raped me. Afterwards, he told me to go back to bed while he left to join the party. His self-hatred was so evident. I wondered, if he couldn't love himself how could he love anyone else? However, he always reassured me that he loved me, and as my father, he was demonstrating his love in this way.

After leaving us, I can't recall my dad ever supporting us financially. I don't remember if he provided food, clothing or anything else for that matter. Honestly, I don't think he did. He could barely provide for himself. There was a time back home, with my abuela and Pucho, when someone stopped by on a motorcycle. I'm not sure who it was, but I believed it was my godfather. However, I might be wrong. He said my father asked him to drop off some lemons. LEMONS! I was looking out through the living room window, perplexed at such a gift. Perhaps he believed his love was the only thing he could give freely – but even at that, he failed miserably.

My dad was not only cruel to me, but he was physically abusive toward my little brother. His new wife had joined him in his cruelty towards us. She, too, was mean and hateful. I am 100% certain that she was aware of what he was doing, she just had to know! I believe she just swept it under the rug or pretended it wasn't happening. She was especially despicable to us. Eventually, she bore him a son and he became their pride and joy, the prince of the house. Unlike the rest of us, they genuinely loved and cared for him. One day, my stepmother asked me to go to his mother's house and get her some bleach because she was washing clothes. My grandma put the bleach in a glass. As I entered the kitchen, his wife was about to drink from the glass and screeched in horror. She then told my father that I had tried to poison her by giving her a glass of bleach to drink! Of course, I got in trouble and my dad beat me up. To be honest, the fact that this woman was dumb enough to have tasted bleach gave me satisfaction and the punishment was worth it. However, it also caused even more misbehaving on my part. All the secrets I carried filled me with guilt and hurt. The hurt turned to anger, and the anger needed an outlet. I became a person with very dark thoughts.

Although we didn't have riches at my maternal grandparents, we lived a pleasant life and we had what we needed: our home was comfortable, clean, and had indoor plumbing and electricity throughout! My dad and his family moved around quite a bit. One of the houses they lived in had no plumbing or electricity and when nightfall arrived we had to use lanterns, the kind of lanterns that you must put oil in. Even their iron was vintage! If our clothes needed ironing, you needed to open the iron's flap and put charcoal inside for it to warm up and function. So many reasons why I despised visiting him.

My father and his family were so poor that their house didn't even have an indoor bathroom, instead, it had an outhouse. Oh, how I hated using the outhouse! It was nasty, smelly, and it became a symbol of anxiety and pain. I knew that if I woke up in the middle of the night to go use the latrine, the monster would also wake up and I would be subjected to his abuse.

One night, I woke up with a full bladder, so I quietly made my way outside petrified to make any noise. I remember walking on my tiptoes afraid that the weight of my entire foot would make noise and wake up the monster. I breathed a deep sigh of relief for I had made it outside and he had not woken. It was so dark out; the only light came from the night sky. I looked up and gazed at the stars that were shining so bright. The sky looked so beautiful; the moon looked huge, and the sounds of critters scurrying around and crickets singing in the night brought me joy! Again, I found myself looking up at the sky to find peace and forget the torments of my life. I stayed outside for a few minutes taking it all in and listening to the sounds of the night, I felt so good. After a few minutes of solitude, I mustered the courage to go back inside and tiptoed my way back to bed. I almost made it; except this time, it wasn't the monster that was waiting for me. It was his wife's brother who got me just before I made it to bed. He took me to the back of the house, and there he had his way with me. I wasn't in much shock as he got on top of me. It was as if I came to expect it. I was looking right past him and again I found myself gazing at the dark sky; the same sky that just a few minutes ago had given me peace. His breathing was labored and intense and it took him what it seemed like an eternity to finish. I stood motionless; like a corpse which was fitting because inside I was dying little by little. He felt so heavy on top of me, and he was looking straight at me; not a hint of shame for what he was doing. Sort of like a hunter staring at his prey just before taking a shot. Once he was done, I put my underwear back on and walked to bed and went to sleep. I don't think I thought of anything, I just slept. Spending time with my father had become hell for me, and I dreaded the thought of our school vacations specifically because we had to go spend time with him!

On another occasion when we went to visit him, my brother, Carlos had gone to shower, and when he came out he had a towel wrapped around his head. When my father saw him, he became enraged and called him explicit, derogatory names and homosexual slurs. He stated only gays or men who wanted to be women would wear a towel around their head. He went on and said if my brother wanted to be a girl he would beat that out of him—and beat him he did. I sat in horror as I watched him beat my brother. I wanted to intervene, but my own survival instinct prevented me. I was terrified of my father. When he was done with the punishment, I rushed to my brother's side to hug him tightly and cry with him. We were sobbing, snot and all. In our hearts, we knew this man hated us.

My father's cruel behavior transcended the bedroom. He took me to work one day and during the bus route I sat behind him. I vividly remember we came to a stop and he looked at me and said, "I know that I am NOT the only one doing what I do to you. I know that there ARE others but I don't care. I love you the most." I was overcome with shame as if a big stain covered me, and now it was visible to others. Since that day, I started to wonder who else could see it? See, back home with my abuelos, I had fallen victim to another predator who was a drug addict consumed by evil. Eventually, his addiction almost cost him his life, and I doubt that a day goes by that he doesn't see the consequences of every bad decision he made. But for me, this was one more secret to carry and these secrets started weighing heavily on me.

As much as I hated going to Cali to spend time with my dad and his family, that is how much I loved being home with my sisters at my grandparents' house. My mom not being able to take care of my little cousin, the one who lost her mom tragically in NY, sent her to Colombia and she too was now being cared for by our grandparents. I was thrilled! That meant another friend for us to play with. We always had so much fun with our friends. We used to walk to El Rio Consota (Consota River), most of the time without adult supervision, for an afternoon of swimming and relaxation. Those were different times! Sometimes our trips to el rio were planned and sometimes they were spur of the moment type of thing. There were many afternoons when some of us in the group would sneak out with an item of food from home and bring it with us; this even included a couple of pots we would use for cooking. At the river, we would take big rocks and wood we found lying around and have a comitiva (prepared, cooked and shared food with friends). It was always a great time. We were carefree and loved spending time with one another in the outdoors.

We played until dark and even at times after dinner, we would go outside and call on each other to sit down to talk about the day's events. Since none of us had a lot, we were very resourceful to figure out what to play and what to use to play our games. We had neither bats nor softballs but that didn't stop us from playing "bate" which was our version of softball. Usually, our bat was whatever big stick we could find and most of the times it was a pretty wide piece of wood, and a ball. Our favorite games were bate, dodgeball, hide and go seek and tug of war. We were always serious about our games and would spend hours playing with friends.

From the outside, you couldn't tell the secret I was carrying and being back at home, I would always forget about my secret life in Cali. With my abuelos, I tried to be as normal as any other kid but beneath, my smiles and my laughter, I was haunted by awful memories of abuse. I had never shared with anyone what I was going through at the hands of my father and the other men. In addition, to my dad's issues, our next-door neighbor in Pereira, an older man, fat man also used to "please" himself at my expense whenever he saw me in our backyard. These moments began to wear on me like blisters from a tight pair of shoes.

Seven years after my mom left, the buzz at home began that we would soon be reunited with her and my oldest sister in the U.S.! My oldest sister had already been with our mom for a couple of years now. She, too, became too much to handle for my grandparents so she was the first one who made her trip to the U.S. I couldn't wait to share the news with my friends. In my innocence, I promised them that I would send them toys and clothes, just like my mom did for us and that we would stay in touch and be friends forever. Suddenly, life was looking up and some of the fog that had plagued my life for the past seven years was lifting and my future looked brighter.

The time we had been waiting for was almost here! I was excited about running errands to get us ready for the upcoming trip and though we did not have too many details about it, it didn't matter. I did not ask any questions. I was happy to get my passport picture taken. I was wearing a cool gray and pink blouse with corduroy brown pants that my mom had sent in one of the boxes we loved to receive all the way from NY. My long straight hair was pulled back with a headband also sent by mom. I stood straight and tried not to smile too big but I couldn't wait to leave so it was so hard not to have a big grin on my face! Now it wasn't just about seeing my mom; it was about escaping the battleground that I felt I was losing. Deep Inside, I was fighting a war.

The last time I went to Cali to see my father did not faze me. I think for the first time since the abuse began, I did not mind going to see him even though I knew what awaited me. I truly didn't care. I had too much to look forward to and nothing would dampen my happiness. There is nothing really memorable about that last trip except that I was sad that I wouldn't see my brother again. I knew that I was escaping hell but my brother had no escape. My father did it again and again and again. It wasn't that I didn't hurt but I finally saw a light at the end of that very dark tunnel.

As we were saying goodbye, my grandma and each of my aunts and uncles told me they loved me and would miss me. I couldn't believe my ears. They did not love me nor would they miss me. For all these years, they turned a blind eye to the abuse I had suffered at the hands of my father! Their brother, their son, had used me to satisfy his disgusting desires and they didn't say a word. Every time I visited my father and his family, the spark in my eyes grew dimmer and dimmer until it was almost gone. Driving away from my father's house, I looked out the window with a sense of relief. Seeing the trees passing by and looking at the road ahead seemed to represent freedom. No longer would I go through the pain or humiliation that had lasted for the last seven years. I was so excited to start a new life with my mom and sisters.

Chapter Five

LEAVING COLOMBIA/
GOD PROVIDES

*"God sends angels with special orders
to protect you wherever you go,
defending you from all harm"
Psalm 91:11*

I couldn't believe it! I was finally going to be with my mom again. For as important as this trip was, I didn't think about how we were going to get there. I just wanted to be with my mom. As we prepared for the trip, I heard my grandma and aunt discussing a "coyote."

"It will take a couple days and a few stops, but they will get there."

Grandma shook her head.

"It is the best way. I'm only concerned if we can trust this coyote."

At the time, I didn't understand what this meant. But it dawned on me as we began our trip, this would not be a typical trip. We would be entering the United States illegally. When my mom travelled to the US, she was smuggled on a boat and arrived in Miami. It wasn't as easy as applying for a visa and getting it approved. Not only did that process cost money that we didn't have but it was extremely hard to get approved. The only way to make it was by taking a chance and trusting a total stranger with our lives. However, our journey would be different than mom's. We were crossing the border between Mexico and the US and though we knew it would take a few days to make it across, if we made it all. I was excited yet scared of the unknowns. We expected it to be an adventure traveling to the United States but that was an understatement.

We left Colombia at about noon time and headed toward Mexico; our first stop: Panama.

I had never been on a plane before and as I settled into my seat, I had flashbacks of my mom boarding the plane when she left for New York. At that moment I wondered if she had been scared? My aunt and her daughter were on this journey with us and it was nice to have her there as the trusted adult. Funny how one can retain certain memories as a child. Once we landed in Panama, I can remember how hot and humid the day was. So much so, that I couldn't wait to be back on the plane. Or perhaps I just wanted to get going on our way to our next stop: Mexico.

We were so excited to arrive in Mexico! We were able to experience another first!! Until then, we had never spent the night in a hotel – AND it had a pool!!! It was also the first time we were unable to make eye contact with anyone. The mere face to face look could divulge who we were and what we were doing. It was too risky, and we didn't want to be sent back to Colombia. Everything was a hush – not the ideal trip for children.

After one night at the hotel, we were back on our journey. Sitting in the back of a cab, I recall looking out the window into the street, my eyes fixing on buildings unlike any I'd seen back in Pereira. After a short drive that seemed like hours, we arrived at someone's house. There were no pleasantries, no greetings of any form. We were hurried through the front door into a big room in the attic. The most shocking part was that the room was already full of people. We were confined to this overcrowded space for several days and our time there was the complete opposite of the hotel. There was no pool, no fancy lobby or anything. There were so many people stuffed in the room, making it muggy and hard to breathe. We slept on mattresses on the floor and were only allowed to leave for trips to the bathroom.

Just imagine, everyone in this house had the same story. During our short stay, we noticed elderly couples, single men and women. There were even several kids who were without any parents. The details may have been a little different, the faces changed, but every one of us shared a common story line: we all were escaping a harsh reality. I think the beauty of this moment was how we all came together. Despite our different backgrounds, the group rallied together to help each other. Some of the adults even "adopted" the unaccompanied kids. At one point, I imagined one of these women could have been like my mom seven years earlier, who left behind her most treasured possession, her three daughters, to search for a better life.

Late on our last night at this house, we were woken up. It was time to move. Without warning, the coyote rushed us out of the house and into the back of a truck. We were split into groups. Ours had about 10 people and though it was a lot of us, there was nothing but silence during this ride. After several hours, the truck came to a stop. Exiting the back of the truck, we saw a rundown house. As we walked toward it, I looked around. We were in the middle of nowhere. The house looked deserted. The windows were dusty, the roof had patched holes in it. Obviously only used for very short stays. The inside didn't look much better. Opening the door, we were greeted by a dark room with a few empty cots scattered across a dirt floor.

Settling with just our backpacks, we tried not to get too comfortable. The truth is, we could only bring what we could carry and light enough that it would not slow us or anyone else down. Sitting in the darkness of this room, it dawned on me that our reality was so uncertain, without notice, we could be on the move again.

Almost immediately after arriving at this location, our coyote gave us instructions on what to expect next. He explained the possible risks of the trip with such a calm demeanor, that we didn't realize the amount of danger that was around us. He taught us to listen for any strange sounds that could signal that a wild animal or other threats were nearby. He mentioned crawling scorpions and actual coyotes in such a nonchalant tone; he seemed totally unphazed by it all. After all, he was a pro who had probably smuggled people across the border many times before. In a monotone voice, he let us know that we would be walking for a few hours through the desert and that we should stay together in order to increase our chances of making it safely to the other side of the river. I was listening intently to remember the warnings and what to do in case of unforeseen turns of events. Closing my eyes and with my hands in praying position, I asked God for protection. Yet, I still couldn't help but be overpowered by a fear of the unknown. I wondered if this trip would work out. Most importantly, I wondered if I would ever see my mom again.

When it was time to go, we grabbed our belongings and headed out the door on the next stretch of our journey. Despite the fact that we had been given extensive instructions, the anticipation and perhaps fear of the unknown shook me. I wondered if I would remember anything that I had just been told. And so, our journey began once again and we found ourselves walking under starry skies for hours. Through it all, I recall looking up to the sky; taking it all in. I pondered whether or not this would work out.

Chapter Six

CROSSING THE RIO GRANDE

*"Look at the splendor of your skies, your
creative genius glowing in the heavens.
When I gaze at your moon and your stars,
mounted like jewels in their settings,
I know you are the fascinating artist
who fashioned it all!"*
Psalm 8:3

The sky looked so beautiful; the stars were so bright that they lit up the way. There was such an adrenaline rush going through my body that it gave me strength when I should have been tired. At one point, we walked along a train track on a gravel road. As instructed, we were careful to listen for strange sounds and to stick close together. Sure enough, we heard a noise—it could have been a wild animal or perhaps someone else trying their luck at crossing the border. Wouldn't you know it, I ended up losing my shoe in sheer panic – it was never found. Sadly, I continued my journey with just one shoe. It didn't stop me; nothing was going to stop me.

After a while the rocks on the road seemed to disappear or maybe my foot just didn't notice anymore. The adrenaline had kicked into overdrive. I was on a quest to see my mom. We continued to walk for hours until we got to the Rio

Grande River. I had expected this river to be like many others I visited with my friends in Colombia. But this river looked nothing like that. This river was very wide and calmer than what I was used to. We inflated a raft and stepped into it. It was still dark but the moonlight casted an unnerving glow on the flowing water and at that moment I became scared. Getting on a raft with many people; wondering if that raft would hold us; was not as scary as the thought of what awaited us once we got to the other side. My feelings did not betray me – I was right to be scared.

"Show me the wonders of your great love,
you who save by your right hand
those who take refuge in you from their foes.
Keep me as the apple of your eye; hide me in the shadow
of your wings"
Psalm 17:7-8

Once we made it across the river, the walking continued. It felt like a game of hide and go seek. We would hide behind bushes while the lights from the border patrol would seek out intruders making their way into this country. My heart never stopped racing since this journey began but now it felt like it was going to pierce through my chest.

It seemed like it had rained in the days leading up to this night for the ground was extremely muddy. My feet were sinking into the mud however, that did not deter me, I was still on my mission. Time and time again we squatted down whenever the light from the border patrol made its way toward us until we finally reached an open road. It was there where we waited for the next leg of our journey to start.

The truck that picked us up was a produce truck full of lettuce heads. We climbed inside through a compartment door and proceeded to the very end of the cargo bed. Since this truck was transporting lettuce, it was refrigerated and pitch-black inside. It was so cold inside that compartment that we were huddled tightly together in an attempt to stay warm. At one point, I had to go to the bathroom very badly, but there was nowhere to go. I told my aunt and she replied, "just pee right there." I had no choice but to do just that! Thank God no one could see me so I bent down and released my bladder. The truck's only stop was the final one stop on this leg of the journey. We then got into another vehicle, which would take us to our next destination for the night. We finally made it to some big house, and we were so tired; we went straight to sleep. No one spoke of that day's events nor said anything for that matter. While I laid on the mattress that was strewn across the floor, I thought of what had transpired and was relieved and grateful that all went well. I was sure that we had been cared for, now I realize that we were protected. GOD's hand had been with us. That night as I thought of this, I fell asleep until the morning light woke me up.

> "You've gone into my future to prepare the way,
> and in kindness you follow behind me
> to spare me from the harm of my past.[a]
> With your hand of love upon my life,
> you impart a blessing to me"
> Psalm 139:5

The next morning, I had a piece of white bread for breakfast and it tasted like heaven, it was so delicious! It was WONDER Bread! Afterwards, we went to a huge supermarket and all the while, my aunt warned us not to look at anyone and to keep our heads down because we didn't blend in. But my twin sister and I were in awe because we had never seen a supermarket that not only sold food but also sold gadgets and clothing. My aunt bought us our first shoes, white sneakers with Velcro. As I write this and think back I realize they were the most hideous sneakers but as a kid–at that moment, they were so beautiful to me. Our first shopping experience in America was at a local Walmart!

A couple of days had passed, and we were that much closer to being with our mom and older sister. I could hardly wait! Finally, the day came to be reunited with mom after seven long years. I had so many emotions and so many thoughts. I was mostly excited and nervous at the same. The day I dreamt about for so long was here. The last time I saw my mom was on my sixth birthday. I couldn't wait to touch her and give her a big hug and plant a kiss on her cheeks! Mostly, I couldn't wait for her to hug and kiss ME because I had missed those so much. When I saw my mom and my oldest sister, it was everything I had imagined. We all cried tears of joy and were grateful because we were back together. Nothing would ever separate us again. However, I was no longer the little girl she had left behind; I was a troubled teenager with a dark secret.

Chapter Seven

LIFE IN NEW YORK

*"O Lord our God, let your sweet beauty rest
upon us and give us favor. Come work with us,
and then our works will endure, and
give us success in all we do"*
Psalm 90:17

Everything had changed. EVERYTHING! Being in New York was a huge adjustment. Living with my mom, we witnessed first-hand how hard she worked. She was still a factory worker but she also found herself working in restaurants as a server. As beautiful as she was, I could tell that the years away from us, working in factories under poor conditions had started to take a toll on her. Mom's eyes looked tired. But despite her crazy work days, her face would brighten every time she saw us.

My mom worked so hard to get us here for a better life; but we had been apart for too many years. There was something missing. Don't misunderstand me, life in my new home with mom was good but honestly, we seemed like strangers – we now knew very little about each other. Being in New York was rather chaotic for us. Even our living space seemed so cramped. We now lived with our mom, her new husband and my two sisters in a one-bedroom apartment in Astoria, Queens. My aunt and cousin spent a couple of days with us. Her son, who had arrived a few years earlier, had come for them. But until then – they slept on the sofa bed in the living room while my sisters and I slept on the floor in the bedroom. Once my aunt left, my twin and I slept on the sofa bed where we spent many nights reminiscing about our lives and friends back in Colombia. When my aunt left, she took the last bit of Colombia with her. I realized how much I missed my country. The chickens in the backyard, the occasional pig that we would fatten up until it was ready to be eaten (especially during the holidays) and my grandpa. How I missed my grandpa! He taught me how to get a chicken ready–from killing it, removing the feathers, and handing it over to my grandma so she could prepare our lunch. There were so many vivid memories that made me immediately miss my home; my Colombia. However, I was doing the best I could to adjust to my new home.

*"He lived by faith as an immigrant in his
promised land as though it belonged to someone else"
Hebrews 11:9*

One morning my mom told us to make breakfast for ourselves. My twin made two eggs for us to share. When mom saw how little there was on our plate, she asked about it.

"I made eggs for me and Claudia–two eggs to share, one for each of us."

A flash of sadness passed on my mom's face; as if a revelation had just taken place. She saw how content we were with so little and realized how we must've lived for the past few years. In that moment, she was determined to make sure we no longer had to ration our food that way. She wanted us to eat as much as we wanted. We especially loved when she baked the Pillsbury Crescent Rolls! We would eat them as soon as they came out of the oven as we sat watching TV. Not yet in school, the TV became our English tutor. Spending so much time in front of the tube, enabled us to learn this new foreign language that at first seemed so confusing. Little by little we were able to piece two and two together and start making sense of the story. Soon, we were able to understand a word here and there until we got what the plot was about.

During this adjustment period, we didn't dare make eye contact with anyone when we were outside. We just couldn't. We thought that if we did – someone would surely know that we were illegal immigrants and that would jeopardize our lives in this country. There was always a fear within me. I was so afraid that my face would be obvious for someone to call me out as a "wetback", an illegal immigrant that was not welcomed in this country. With time, the more I became comfortable in my surroundings, the less fearful I became. Gradually, my fear was replaced by the excitement of being in this country; I started to become alive.

"... he who appoints the sun to shine by day,
who decrees the moon and stars to shine by night,
who stirs up the sea so that its waves roar—
the Lord Almighty is his name"
Jeremiah 31:35

My mom and her husband made plans to take us to the beach over one weekend. It would be my first time at the beach and I couldn't wait to get there! Up until now, I had only seen it on the television and the joy I felt anticipating my feet sinking in white sand and swimming in crystal blue waters, was more than I could describe. I kept thinking *how much longer? How far is this beach?* Although it was only 30-40 minutes away, it seemed like forever! When we arrived, to my dismay–it was not what I had seen on TV. It was nothing like Miami Vice, which we watched together with my abuela. The water was not blue as I had expected, and it definitely was not warm. Still, we were just so happy to be there for the first time and swim in the ocean. I was cautious to stay close and not wander too far. Truth is that the ocean scared me; so big and some parts seemed so deep. As I stood there I looked as far as my eyes could see and for the first time since arriving here, I was able to relax. What a sight! The sky and water colliding and becoming one. One of the very first glimpses of the wonder of my creator.

On another Saturday mom took us to Steinway Street in Queens to go shopping as the school year was getting closer. What a nice place that was! We walked by clothing store after clothing store. We mostly stopped to window shop, but some stores we went inside. To this day, my mom still loves to window shop. One store we saw was named "Strawberry" and the window display was so beautiful that we decided to go inside to pick out a couple of outfits. Leaving that store we went to a store called "Mandee" and picked out an outfit that fit just right. This was so amazing. All that shopping and walking made us so hungry that we stopped to eat at a pizzeria. It was my first time eating Italian pizza and I did not like it at all. It tasted so weird! Where was the pineapple and ham? This pizza only had cheese and red sauce. It was not very appetizing, but I was so hungry that I ate it. *I might as well get used to this different food*, I thought to myself.

Life was good and I began to enjoy my new normal. However, at nightfall I laid in my bed and my mind relived the nights of abuse at the hands of my father. It was as if these memories would wait until night to haunt me. I struggled to reconcile with these thoughts. I blamed myself for all those years that I endured his sexual abuse.

Why didn't I speak up? Was it that I enjoyed it? Or was it really the terror that my dad would go through with his threats and find a way to kill my mom? Why didn't I resist going for vacation; then I would not have to spend time with him and his family? Was it truly my fault? As I battled in my head, I would recall the sick words he murmured after he was done with me. They played in the back of my mind like an old record. *"I do this because I love you."* It was during this time that my self-esteem began to dwindle, and the blame was a real voice inside my heart. Everything became even darker. I would imagine the day I would go back to tell him how much I despised him. I wanted him to know my deep disdain for him. I hated him. I played the same scenario in my head, if he would ever need help; even be a beggar on the street, I would surely walk right pass him and not even look back. The depth of my pain would further playout the scene as in a movie; if he would ever be sick or helpless, I would spit in his face.

In addition to the thoughts of my dad that plagued me, the images of the obese, disgusting neighbor tormented me as well. The one who lived next door with his wife. Every day as he saw us playing in the backyard, he would expose himself. He was a man engulfed in perversion. He was obviously fighting his own demons as he enjoyed preying on little girls. The anger was taking on a life of its own. My thoughts birthed even more anger than before; but I contained it inside and did not allow anyone to see it, especially my mom. After all, she was clueless to what had occurred. I became a person with two different lives. One life of horrible secrets that I, alone, had access to. The other was the public one. I had mastered the ability to put up a front for all to see.

One day while mom was out at work, my twin and I were rummaging through the apartment. We weren't looking for anything in particular just bored and curious. We found some papers and letters so we began reading through them. First, we found newspaper clippings – lots of them – describing how my aunt had died. We were horrified! After that, we also found a few letters from my dad. His letters to my mom were full of lies. He wrote how much he was doing for us and how he was taking care of us financially. He mentioned that he was sending school supplies among other things. He portrayed himself as a heavenly saint. My twin and I were both in shock! We could not believe what we were reading. My hatred towards him deepened even more. He was a despicable human being uncapable of love, affection and even telling the truth.

Chapter Eight

SCHOOL LIFE

*"My deep need calls out to the
deep kindness of your love.
Your waterfall of weeping sent waves of
sorrow over my soul, carrying me away,
cascading over me like a thundering cataract"
Psalm 42:7*

When mom announced that she had enrolled us in school, I did not know what to expect. I could feel the anxiety arise because I didn't speak English. I was worried that I wouldn't be able to make friends. But my worries were unfounded – not the case at all.

The first day of class was unforgettable. It seemed as though everyone in class was similar to us. Some spoke broken English while others, like us, hardly spoke English at all. It was amazing because it was the first time I met so many kids from different parts of the world! There was the girl from Egypt with a sweet smile accentuated by her braces. There was the shy girl and the chubby boy from Greece who was a showoff. The boy from Colombia whom eventually I developed a crush on. His good friend from Puerto Rico that my twin eventually developed a crush on. The sheepish Indian girl who hardly spoke up and the list went on and on and then there was us.

Our teachers were nice and some had more compassion than others and tried to make the students feel like they belonged. It was clear that we were in the English as a Second Language (ESL) class. Life as a middle schooler wasn't easy but it wasn't so bad. We met a group of girls that became our instant friends. They spoke Spanish but their first language was English, so they helped my twin and I with translation. They would even write the lyrics of songs we liked so we could sing along with them.

The Greek chubby boy, Peter, began teasing me. Every time the teacher would turn around, he would throw spitballs at me. I asked him many times to stop but he didn't. Reaching the peak of my patience, I picked up my chair and threw it at him. Shockingly, he stood up in anger and I as well not falling for his intimidation tactics. I was ready to fight him off; he had no idea who he was messing with. Hence, my first trip to the principal's office and the first phone call (of many) that my mom would receive.

We soon discovered that life as a middle schooler at I.S. 10 Horace Greeley would be adventurous! There were many days we would cut school with our friends and get on the train with no particular destination in mind. Some days we went to the beach and other days we would just go back to the house with our newfound friends to hang out. We always made it a point to be back at school by the end of the day. We were not considered popular but, in my mind, I was pretty cool. I was making the transition from a girl who hardly looked at anyone's face to a girl who was now ready for the world.

As the weather started warming up and we went outside for recess, a tall dark, not so handsome boy began to come around with friends during our lunch period. Although my experience with men was not so great, he made me feel special. He was very friendly and would constantly flirt with me. He then began waiting for me after school and we would talk and listen to music. Our favorite song to listen to was Spring Love by Stevie B. We listened to the whole album but kept Spring Love on repeat. Our friendship had turned romantic.

On one occasion, my mom gave my twin and I money to hold with the intention to send it to Colombia for my abuelos. My twin put it in her backpack. That evening my mom asked for the money and we could not find it. We frantically searched but it was gone; my mom was furious. She had every right to be upset; she worked so hard so my abuelitos could receive her financial support. We had misplaced the money, now we could not be trusted. My aunt happened to be visiting. Rather than help ease the situation, she escalated it – making it really worse. She told my mom that we had probably used that money to get an abortion. My mom jumped on that wagon quickly and wouldn't listen as we told her that my aunt was lying. My aunt hadn't always been nice but why was she making these accusations now was unknown to me. We were not sexually active. She was a liar and we were deeply hurt; so, we ran away.

Running away for the day became part of our life. I remember we did that quite often. This time, we went to Jose's house, the not so handsome boy I was seeing. I had become good friends with his sister also. His family was humble and welcoming and always made me feel at home whenever I went to visit. But that relationship soon faded away and we decided to just be friends.

I was happy at school and soon realized that life as a teenager in the U.S. was very different than back in Colombia. We no longer went out to play with friends but now our new friends held house parties with older kids and music with beats and rhythms that was played so loud we couldn't hear each other talk. These were house parties with low lights and smoke machines that were frequent, but we seldom enjoyed. Quite often we helped set up for the party but since our curfew was 10 pm, the parties were just getting started as we were leaving. One time my sister and I lost track of time and mom came for us. I was mortified! She was so upset; she wouldn't listen to anything we had to say.

During this time, we had befriended a girl name Erica; she was not that popular but definitely more popular than we were. She was in her last year of middle school and had already started making friends with high schoolers from Bryant High School down the block from our middle school. I can't remember exactly what changed but the following year Erica started High School, she became a different person and turned mean to us. It was as though she had something to prove. She had new friends and her popularity became obvious. Perhaps all the parties her mom allowed elevated her on the popularity scale. One of her new friends, for unknown reasons, really disliked us. Nothing in particular had ever occurred between us. She was just a bully looking for an easy target. Usually after school she would yell mean things to us. For fear of making waves since it was "obvious" that I was an illegal immigrant, I kept walking. Her "wetbacks" chant made it all the more a terrifying reality that folks knew I was illegal, and I would be sent back to Colombia. I kept quiet but deep down I felt more upset. One cold day as my twin and I were walking home with some friends, all of a sudden this gal pushed me and I fell to the ground. I was so angry! I looked up to see that Erica was with her; they were both laughing. My anger turned to hurt. Hurt to see a friend now become an enemy. The group of girls we were with had some words with them and they walked away.

A couple of days later, we decided to cut school again. Instead of riding the train with our friends we decided to walk back to our home. It was a good day; we talked and laughed and watched TV until it was time for the last class, then we walked our friends back to school. We were almost there when we encountered Erica and her new friend, the bully. It was evident they were looking for a fight. When I saw there were more of them, my heart sank but it was time to stand my ground. They came toward us and as the bully approached me, hands in her pockets, she said she wanted to fight. I was actually happy, after all, I knew how to hold my own with many other fights in my past. I told her that I would fight – but it was to be a clean fight – no weapons!

Fighting in the U.S. was very different. Unlike in Colombia, kids here would make weapons out of wires from notebooks using them as rings that cut through the skin. They also spread Vaseline on their faces like spreading butter on toast so the punches roll off. Heavy rings on almost every finger; and blades in between and you'd better have a watchful eye because before you knew it, the blades were taken out if you weren't looking. I remember one time a girl was hiding a blade in her mouth. What a skill to have! Through fighting, I had finally found an outlet for all the years of repressed anger due to all the abuse. I demanded that this bully remove her hands from her pocket; as she did, there was a ring on every finger that I demanded she remove. She was a dirty fighter! I didn't have time to get ready though, couldn't put Vaseline on my face nor put my hair up because as soon as she took her rings and jacket off, we went at it. I had so much anger inside and all I wanted to do was make her pay for how mean she had been. We threw punches and pulled hair for what seemed like forever. Once I had her on the ground, on her back, I punched her face nonstop and she grabbed my left arm and bit me so hard and so deep that the scar remains even today. When we heard the police sirens, she let go. I stood up and I kicked her so hard with my winter boots, she let out a scream. We took off running as the cops got out of their cars. That was terrifying! I was sure that the cops would come knocking at the door of our tiny apartment. I was so afraid that I would be on my way back to Colombia in no time. When we got home, I hid under the blankets with the lights off. When mom arrived from work, she was concerned that I was in bed. As any nurturing mother would do, she came to see that I was ok but when she picked up the blanket, she saw the bite on my arm and I had to explain what had transpired. She was visibly upset.

The next day during school, we had a strong feeling that the fight would continue. We anticipated that this bully and her friends would come looking for us before the last class let out. I recall looking out the window, a bundle of nerves, when I saw what seemed like the whole entire high school waiting outside of our school. My heart was racing!

When we got outside, the bully approached us once again; without hesitation she said she was there to finish what was started the day before. However, this time, my twin got in between us and said: "Today is my turn!"

With pride I thought *that's my sister!* We still had each other's back and she was so ready to take her down. Unfortunately, my twin sister was too eager to fight and failed to ask this bully to take her hands out of her pocket. Before you knew it, the bully took a combination padlock, probably from her locker and hit my sister several times on her head until she bled; it wasn't too bad – but I was ready to kill this girl. Just before I approached the fight, the teachers came out and so did the cops, again. We were taken into the principal's office where they called my mom to tell her what had transpired. She was fuming with anger and lectured us on our walk home. We could tell she was sick and tired of getting complaints from school.

Right before the school year ended, in the classroom closet we found a box full of blank certificates. Jackpot! What better way to butter up mom than to bring home certificates of recognition? We pulled out a few of those blank certificates and had one of our friends write our names and sign them; we brought them home to mom. She was so proud! It wasn't that we were bad students; we always got good grades but we never earned those certificates of merit. I believe it was all the chaos we usually caused in class.

Over the summer, I met a boy named Derek from the neighborhood. I was smitten by him. He had a sweet nature and brought a different kind of excitement into my life. Derek was soft spoken; somewhat funny but mostly, very caring and tender. One afternoon, we ended up back at his mom's place and had sex. That was the first time I willingly had sex with anyone, yet I did not enjoy it. Finally, I had to face the questions I had asked myself many times when I laid in bed: *Why didn't I tell my dad to stop? Was I powerless and he was my dad?* A dad that although did not respect me, still I had to show respect. No, I did not enjoy it no matter what the voices in my head kept telling me. I was finally starting to understand the impact the abuse was having on my life. Eventually, I grew tired of Derek and did not want to see him again but I didn't have the heart to tell him. However, my twin was more than happy to do so. When he came to visit, I hid at the top of the stairs and watched and she broke the news to him. Poor Derek; he had not seen that coming and was visibly upset. I was unaware of the pattern that was unfolding – I pushed away nice boys because I didn't feel I was worthy of their attention.

The opportunity for a clean slate! We started high school at the International High School at La Guardia Community College. Our mom made it clear that she was not to get any more phone calls from the principal; we had to shape up. The school was quite large. The high school occupied the first floor – college classes were in the upper floors. Most of the campus was shared.

Chapter Nine

MEETING "T"

The first week of class I was captivated by a young man who was two grades ahead of me. They called him "T" (short for Tomas). He was popular, very funny, a fashionable dresser, and a bit full of himself. Everyone wanted to be his friend. Before I knew it, we were a couple; I had no idea T was a player. He was what I understood as my first love.

High School seemed like a whole new ball game; my twin and I had never been in separate classes. It took a bit to get used to not having my best friend in the room. I was a bit anxious and timid at first but that didn't last long because, as identical twins, we realized we could switch classes to be with our boyfriends; I with T and she with Edgar. The new season had its luster – but I was still that troubled girl with an attitude, capable of rage and struggling with depression. What I truly enjoyed about this high school was that everyone was from different countries and English was a second language for all of us. Perhaps because we had so much in common – we made friends very quickly.

During this season, I also changed my look. I traded my leggings and fitted blouses for baggy jeans and oversized shirts; boots replaced my sneakers. Hair in a ponytail, hoop earrings and red lipstick that reminded me of my abuela. I looked forward to school although I continued to cut classes with my boyfriend and his friends. My intention was to be like my friends who seemed so cool. My girlfriends were self-assured and had the appearance that displayed confidence in who they were. "They were comfortable in their own skin" – at least that's how I saw them.

I enjoyed my time with T and his family and would rather spend my time there than in my own home. Each day, my love for him grew deeper and even though my mind warned me many times as did my mom, my heart did not listen. Eventually, we did have sex and still I did not enjoy it; I laid there motionless waiting for him to finish. Whether his parents knew what went on behind the locked bedroom, I will never know. But they never gave any notion that it was a big deal. T was very well liked by most of his neighborhood and was the most popular of his friends. As we walked to his home, folks would call out his name and ask if they were hanging out? Or if he would be around later? I got to know some of his friends and soon discovered that they belonged to what seemed like a gang.

By now, we had moved in with my mom's boyfriend whom she met at a restaurant where she worked. He was kind and genuinely caring; he always introduced us as his daughters to everyone we met and that felt good. Is this how a loving father behaves? A few months later, his four daughters joined us from the Dominican Republic. We became instant friends. We were a household of 8 living in a 2- bedroom, 1-bathroom home. We had a lot of fun together in our cramped home and we hardly ever complained. As most teenagers; we spent many nights laughing, listening to music and talking about boys. We all had friends in common. My boyfriend, T, would come visit once in a while and met some of our neighborhood friends. As soon as my friends found out where T lived, they became a bit wary. There was bad blood between his neighborhood, Woodside, and my neighborhood, Corona. Still, we all hung out together listening to loud music and talking teen nonsense.

Rosa, a friend I met at school was a complete "bad ass" so I thought. Her "don't mess with me" attitude was way tougher than mine. She was not pretty at all, but confidence made her attractive and I envied that. I would see her in the hallway and light up and soon my admiration for her turned into a little girl crush. It wasn't her looks but her courage that made me want to be around her. She was my first crush on another girl and though this feeling was something new, I kind of liked it. It gave me something else to think about whenever the feelings of insecurity would rise to the surface. Trust me, I was always wondering if people could tell I had been sexually abused but were not letting on. It felt pretty depressing but I was determined to not allow my past define me. As I look back – I realize that it was too late. I was a product of abuse and there was nothing typical about "my normal" at all.

"But the wicked are like the storm-tossed sea, whose restless waves are never still, stirring up mud and mire"
Isaiah 57:20

Around the Christmas holidays, my friend Rosa invited me to hang out after school. She introduced me to a few of her friends; one of them was nicknamed "Porkchop" and another was Steven. I was so excited to meet them, and we immediately clicked. After Chinese food for dinner, we decided to go for a walk – but soon things just did not seem right. I had this feeling in the pit of my stomach that things were not right, yet I pushed those feelings away. Rosa and my two new friends were having conversations on the side that I could not make out. It was as if they were talking in code. I couldn't shake off the uneasy feeling, but I kept walking trying to maintain their pace as they started walking really fast. I saw a woman walking with her son and they were carrying shopping bags; clearly, they had just finished some Christmas shopping. Before I could react, Porkchop got in my face and told me what was about to go down. She told me that we were going to "jump them" and take their shopping bags. My job was to grab the mom's purse – I froze. How I regretted disregarding the feeling that just a minute earlier warned me something was not right. I should've gone home. I did not know what to do… Porkchop got in my face, threatened me and I got scared. This girl that I just met had turned into a monster, barking orders at me. I was so used to reacting that I did what she said. I became a coward – I didn't stand up to her. As the mom and son walked past us, Rosa, Porkchop and Steve jumped them and took their bags and Porkchop looked at me. I grabbed the purse and took off running. I ran and did not stop. I didn't even care to meet up with them; I did not want to be around them at all. I was in a panic thinking the cops must be patrolling looking for me; I jumped on the train and went to my older sister's house.

> "Don't follow after the wicked
> ones or be jealous of their wealth.
> Don't think for a moment they're better off than you.
> ² They and their short-lived success will
> soon shrivel up and quickly fade away
> like grass clippings in the hot sun"
> Psalm 37:1-2

My heart was pounding like a jackhammer and I kept replaying the events in my mind. When I was on the train, I opened the purse to retrieve the wallet. I wanted to see who it belonged to as if knowing the identity of the owner would somehow change anything. I had no intention to return it – I just couldn't risk being arrested. Aside from the woman's ID, the wallet was empty. Poor mom had spent all she had on Christmas gifts and now, because of us, her holiday was ruined. I was mortified. I did the most unimaginable! *How could I do such a thing? Why did I not walk away? Why did I not stand up for myself when Porkchop barked orders at me?* I felt worthless; like garbage, the worst kind of human being. I had crossed a line I never thought I would; I felt ashamed. As I got off the train, I threw the purse in the garbage and ran until I reached my sister's place. When I arrived there, I broke down and cried. I didn't mention what I had done nor did my sister ask. I stayed there for a little bit and then went home. The events of the day kept me up all night. The terrified look of these two poor victims kept flashing in my mind, tormenting me, I couldn't sleep – I deserved that. I remember asking God to forgive me but, how could He? Surely, He despised me. His wrath was coming. Even decades later, I think of that heinous act and wish I had walked away. Rosa and I never discussed what we had done, nor did she ask me to hang out with her ever again.

My mom worked evenings and after she would leave for work, we would wait until we heard our stepdad snoring to sneak out the window to hang out some more. The days just seemed too short for us and we wanted to be free. Night after night, we snuck out the bedroom window and sat outside continuing unfinished conversations from earlier in the day. A few times in the summer, we would stay out all night only to return home before my mom arrived from her overnight shift. We lived for the moment; not fazed by the future; college was not something I thought of much.

I loved my neighborhood and the friends I had and for the moment, life was good! I thought of myself as an average teenager. Although we had moved to a new place with new friends, I was still finding any reason to fight. One late afternoon mom went to answer the door bell. As she opened the front door, a group of girls came inside to finish a fight. Before I knew it, we were punching each other right there in the doorway. My poor mom almost fainted! I bet this was not the life she had expected with us. Still in my mind, I was just a typical girl. One Halloween, while both my mom and stepdad were out of the house, we started an egg fight with our friends that ended up inside our home. We had to cleaned it up before our parents returned. They never found out or at least never mentioned anything.

"And the path of peace they have not known."
Romans 3:17

Out of the blue, T broke up with me and my heart shattered into tiny pieces. I felt as if God had punished me for all that I had done wrong. It had to be – I was dying inside. I would lock myself in the room and cry until I was out of tears. The pain so raw, it physically hurt. I would play the same songs over and over again, torturing myself. I was out of sorts thinking I could not live without him. My mom perhaps was relieved that my relationship had ended; she wasn't impressed by T. She knew too well what I was going through… She also knew I would survive this pain and reminded me that no one dies of a broken heart. However, I was certain I wouldn't survive my pain. I wrote many love letters that he never read; I poured my heart out, pleading for a second chance; not understanding why I was no longer good enough. I would pick up the phone to listen to the ring tone making sure it was still working in case he would reconsider and call. I began seeing another boy; similar to T in many ways yet different. He was handsome and sweet and not full of himself like my ex; not a typical boy who would also be in a gang. Yet soon as T called, I went back to him like a little dog who returns to its master and just in time for school to start.

I was happy to see my friends back at school. I tried joining different clubs at school but that was short-lived. My behavior escalated again. I was disrespectful to my teachers and my peers. My mom was beyond tired of the phone calls from school. She was stressed not only by me and also from her own relationship which was dwindling. After mom and stepdad split up, we moved into a tiny studio apartment. We figured out a routine that suited the three of us. Mom still worked nights while my twin and I slept on the sofa bed. In the morning, mom would arrive, and we were on our way to school. Sometimes as we returned from school, we would take the small TV to the bathroom to not disturb my mom while she slept. We spent hours in the bathroom watching our favorite shows.

A couple of months later, I missed my monthly period. At first, I didn't think anything of it. I hadn't realized the depth of situation; I had just turned sixteen. It was when I began craving ham and cheese sandwiches for breakfast that I began to "freak out" suspecting that I was pregnant. All the questions began to inundate my mind. I was too young. *What am I supposed to do with a child? Where do I go?* Surely my mom would kick me out of the house. I talked to my boyfriend–he was not ready to be a father; I decided to terminate the pregnancy. There was really no question; I had no choice. I looked through the yellow pages and found an abortion clinic. I explained my situation and made an appointment. I was given instructions; they persuaded me to believe that due to the early stages, it was just a mere fetus. Their description had dehumanized the baby. Their words were intentional to remove any guilt about the abortion – they assured me it was not a baby, not yet. Obviously, that made me feel better in a way. I talked to T about what I had learned. I also shared how afraid I was perhaps seeking comfort. I asked if he was coming with me, but he said he couldn't. I was hurt but did not get mad at him; this was not his fault; I blamed myself for the pregnancy. I was truly shaken up. The appointment was a week away... I lived in agony! My sister was the only one who could comfort me. My mom had no clue what I was going through; the thought of telling her never crossed my mind. I already knew, she had made it crystal clear that if I got pregnant, I wouldn't be allowed to stay; sadly, I had no place to go.

At the moment, I was sure I was doing the right thing. My hormones were out of control, and it was so easy for me to hate myself for being so careless and stupid for getting pregnant. How dumb of me! I couldn't look at myself in the mirror without feeling disgusted; perhaps it was also the shame. I believed I deserved everything I was going through. In fact, I was perfectly fine with the idea that if I went to sleep and didn't wake up, I deserved to die!

That dark place I had been living in, was closing in on me – I could hardly breathe. Secretly, I was hurting myself. When I would agonize with my internal pain, I began pulling my hair and hitting myself. Perhaps it made me feel better knowing that I was physically acting out what was going inside – and that subsided some of my internal pain. But the truth was that inside of my body I was growing a human being and despite what I was told, my heart and my mind, knew that there was this tiny baby inside of me and I was going to terminate its life. Another life experience to add to my resume. There were many nights when I laid in bed gazing at my belly and immediately distracting myself to detach from reality. However, this consumed my thoughts. My boyfriend never mentioned it nor was he concerned about the implications of what I was experiencing. It was just another man in my life who had failed me, whose feelings betrayed me. Still, I blamed myself – this was my fault. After all, it was my body.

The day arrived and I was grateful that I was not alone. My sister and her boyfriend came with me. After checking in, my name was called. I was taken into a small room where they took a quick look via a sonogram. I was not allowed to look at the screen, perhaps they figured I would see the heartbeat. Maybe they didn't want me to change my mind and not proceed. The nurse came in and explained the procedure and said that I would not feel a thing. I was then taken into another room where the doctors extracted the "fetus."

I laid on that bed and watched the whole thing unfold before my eyes. I realized that something inside me was dying as well. I believed I was going straight "to hell" perhaps not in a literal sense, but definitely a hell in my soul. When the process was completed, I was given a cup of apple juice and crackers as the nurse looked at me and told me what a good girl I had been. After a little while, I was able to go home. When we stepped outside this clinic, there were people out there with signs that confirmed what I was feeling. I was a murderer. I saw pictures of unborn babies, signs that mentioned God's creation and so much more. I didn't want to read them, but I couldn't look away;

it crushed me. Now, my mind went back to the earlier thoughts when I was laying on the gurney, except that after reading signs calling me a killer, I knew that I was going to spend eternity in the actual hell. At that moment, I felt alone with my pain, in agony. Like I had been dragged across the pavement by my hand. Pain that came to life in the form of tears. *What had I done?* It was rush-hour and the train on our way home was packed. I was standing up for the entire ride and was feeling very weak and scared that my legs would give out. In my guilt, I felt like everyone was aware of where I had been and what I had just done. I felt as if this heinous act I committed was written all over my face and all these strangers despised me. I could not wait to get home. When we finally made it, I went to lie down and gave my mom some excuse as I closed my eyes and cried myself to sleep. I stayed there nursing my wounds until the next day. But more was going on in my heart than I wanted to admit.

Chapter Ten

CHANGES

*"For we are not fighting against flesh-and-blood enemies,
but against evil rulers and authorities of the unseen world,
against mighty powers in this dark world, and against
evil spirits in the heavenly places"*
Ephesians 6:12

At the end of my sophomore year my mom broke the news that we were moving to Long Island, NY. Her commute to work during the night using a shared ride service just became too much for her. It was just too much time away; relocating made so much sense. I was pretty upset about the move, but I understood that my mom would be closer to her job. She gave us a pep talk about this new chapter and encouraged us to be better. This was a chance to reinvent ourselves at the new school. She also warned us about getting any more calls from school. She was totally fed up and we didn't blame her. I had only been trouble, more of a burden since I arrived from Colombia; very far from the joy my mom expected! If only she knew the secrets I'd been carrying; she would surely understand. I wanted to let it all out; to talk to her about the abuse I experienced at the hands of my dad. She had the right to know how much that changed me and how painfully bruised I felt deep inside. I wanted to let her know about the pregnancy but I just couldn't. We did not have that kind of relationship. We weren't close nor were we friends by any means. Every time I contemplated our relationship, it would make me so sad. There was a time that I longed to be with her; how I missed her when there were thousands of miles between us. I would dream of a perfect life. In my mind, our relationship would pick right up from when I was six years old – not this teenager tainted by abuse and dysfunction.

We moved to Glen Cove, Long Island. Our house was beautiful and huge in comparison to every other place we had lived. My twin and I shared a spacious room. Living arrangements didn't matter; heck the size of the room didn't matter as long as we were together. There was something about this move that brought many emotions. I liked the house and the town seemed pretty. Perhaps it was the distance from my boyfriend and my friends. In order to go see them the trip would require both a bus and a train ride.

However, I was excited about the prospect of making new friends. The first day of school, a few seemed to be curious about the twins who had transferred from Queens. Some were nice but not everyone wanted to be our friends. Our new High School was very different. Unlike our other school it was not just for non-native English speaking kids nor made up of kids from other countries, it was a typical American public school with kids from all walks of life.

I couldn't really relate to most kids and this added to my stress and anxiety level but we survived the first few days without major issues. We were learning how to get around school, adjusting to our new classes and in the process, we made a couple of friends. One day while in our free period, I was in the library pretending to read a book, there was a group of kids that could not resist teasing the new girls. I can't recall exactly what was said but it was mean and rude. I tried not to let it bother me, but I couldn't resist. My blood started to boil and at that moment all I wanted to do was beat them up. The thought of being bullied again in a new school was not an option. Before I knew it, a chair went flying through the air, breaking the glass window on the door. UGH! Not even two weeks and we found ourselves in the principal's office – suspended for three days. In order for us to be allowed back, my mom needed to contact the school. I felt like a loser knowing that I would again be a disappointment to my mom. There was no way we would let her find out. We needed a plan ASAP – what to do about that phone call? Luckily, one of our new friends offered to call the school and pretend she was my mom. The next morning, as my mom arrived from work, she noticed we were still in bed. We explained that the school had planned a three-day school trip some time ago and since we were new – it was too late to sign up to go. I had become a good liar or at least in this instance I hid it well – no questions asked.

Meanwhile, my boyfriend and I had adapted to this new normal and were making our relationship work. I would take the long hour plus ride to go see him and he would also come to visit me often as well. Every once in a while, he would come to see me and stay for the night, "on the couch", of course. My mom was pretty naïve, trusting that nothing was happening under the same roof. Once she went to bed, he and I would have sex. It seemed I had no moral values and didn't respect my mom's rules. Looking back, I didn't think I was doing anything wrong. After all, growing up, this sort of thing always happened at night after everyone else was asleep. Soon after I became pregnant a second time. I was devastated. I began punishing myself. I hit myself, bit myself, even pulled my own hair trying to numb the feelings I was going through. *How could I be so stupid???* How did I convince myself that this could never happen again; we were not using birth control. I knew what I had to do because despite the fact that I was rebellious, I was terrified of my mom. I made a couple of phone calls; connected with a Social Worker who helped me through the entire process of having an abortion all over again. I still remembered the feelings after my first abortion. I had felt like the biggest failure ever and here I was again, seeing that as the only way out rather than facing the consequences of my actions. I cried every day. This time the pain, anxiety and depression had intensified.

The Social Worker accompanied me to a doctor's appointment. As they were performing the ultrasound, I was looking at the screen trying to decipher the image of the baby. When the technician noticed, she turned the screen away and said she was going to get the doctor. The doctor came in looked at the screen, took some notes and walked back to her office. Once the ultrasound was completed, I met with her. She asked me if I had been spotting. I replied yes. How long? Almost from the beginning. I described what I saw each time I went to the bathroom. After a few more questions, she indicated that my pregnancy was not normal; she called it a Molar pregnancy. She explained that even if I decided to stay pregnant, the baby would never come to full term. I began to cry in her office and the Social Worker held my hand. She was very kind to me. On our drive back to her office, she mostly spoke because I was crying. She said that in a way, this was a blessing in disguise and that now I had no choice but to terminate the pregnancy. Her words did not bring me comfort.

*"Forgive my failures as a young man,
and overlook the sins of my immaturity"*
Psalm 25:6

After the procedure and as time had gone by, I felt less guilt since I would not have been able to keep the baby. I convinced myself that I had NO choice. I was given birth control and I had to conceal it. One day as I was watching TV, my mom found the pills while she was cleaning. She confronted me about it. In a panic, I told her that it wasn't mine and when she wouldn't let up, I called her crazy. Next thing I felt was the broom she was holding broken over my head. She was enraged. I was so disrespectful. *How was it that our relationship was in such disarray that I couldn't bring myself to trust my mom with what was going on in my life?* I always felt so alone. I longed to have a good relationship with her. I just didn't know how to. A couple of months later my mom had given me permission to go with my boyfriend to the beach along with friends from the youth group he attended once in a while. The morning finally came and I was so excited; I had been looking forward to this trip. As I got ready, my mom arrived home from work and asked me where I was going. She had forgotten that she had given me permission to go. When I was about to leave to catch the bus to Queens, my mom changed her mind and said I couldn't go because I hadn't earned it. I was furious and told her that I WAS going. That resulted in a huge argument; she said if I left the house, I should take my clothes because I wouldn't be welcomed back.

In disbelief, I put some of my things in a bag and walked out seeming unfazed by what just occurred. After the beach, I stayed at my boyfriend's house. Two weeks later, my mom gave me an ultimatum. Come back home with her and straighten out; go back to Colombia; or if I didn't choose either of those, she would call the police and report me as a runaway. I chose to go back to Colombia. I went home to Long Island to wait until it was time to return to my native country. I don't know if that was the answer she expected or it was the easiest way to scare me back home; regardless, I knew this is what I wanted to do. In the days that followed until my trip, my mom and I hardly spoke. In a way I was relieved, it seemed that all I did was disappoint her and there was nothing I could say to change her view of me. Though I was somewhat sad that I would miss my boyfriend, it did not compare to how I felt for leaving my twin behind. However, I knew that it would be just for a little while because soon I would be getting my green card and would be able to return to the US.

> *"Where could I go from your Spirit?*
> *Where could I run and hide from your face?"*
> *Psalm 139:7*

I was thrilled to be back in Colombia! It was amazing to see and spend time with my childhood friends that I missed so much. Despite all of the pain that I endured as a little girl, my childhood in Colombia was filled with great memories and I looked forward to making up for lost time with my friends. The truth is that a lot had in fact changed. I had grown up and so had my friends; some had moved away to either Spain, London or the U.S. It was good to catch up with those who remained. Almost immediately after reconnecting with some, the partying began. I had friends whose friends owned fincas (country homes) that were beautiful with big pools and game rooms and we would spend many weekends there. I would tell my grandma about my plans to spend the weekend at a friend's house and with whom—it wasn't an issue. The weekends were wild with drinking and dancing parties and sex; always meeting new people. I am not proud of the things that occurred at these parties; looking back, I wish my grandma would have stopped me, but I don't know if I would have listened anyway.

At times the rage within surfaced to remind me it had followed me to Colombia. One time, I was visiting a friend and as we talked about reuniting with family back in the U.S. an unwelcomed gal came in; she was a relative's girlfriend and also seemed to be a "call girl." After an intense conversation outside had turned into a yelling match, my rage surfaced. So much so that it was almost impossible for her to get out from under me. When someone finally managed to pull me away from her, I told her that next time she went looking for trouble she should do her homework first. During my walk home, I replayed the events that took place earlier in the day. I was proud of myself for holding my own. My fighting was so frequent I had become quite skillful at it and this was a good thing because trouble seemed to follow me everywhere.

I wanted to be independent and hated the thought of asking my mom for money. I decided to look for work and quickly found a job at a very popular shoe store. I enjoyed my time with my coworkers, and we spoke about our future. I continued going out with friends to clubs and bars and went out on dates here and there. I had little self-respect for neither myself nor my body. I struggled with moral values. Sex was just an act of satisfying one's desires and had nothing to do with love nor spiritual embrace.

Soon, I began to spend time with my uncle's wife and my cousins. One of their relatives owned a beautiful finca outside of the city. There, I met a man who was seventeen years my senior. He was unlike anyone I had ever met before; he was a successful man and had his life together. During one of our trips to the finca, a group of us spent the day drinking, eating and listening to music; it was lots of fun! All throughout the day, this man and I kept glancing at each other and played flirtatious games from afar. After calling it a night I went to sleep exhausted. As I laid in bed going over the day's events and rehashing the not so innocent flirting between me and that older man; all of the sudden the door opened up and he came in to "checkup" on me. That is how our relationship began. It felt magical and perhaps because it was forbidden it made it more intriguing not to get caught. It wasn't only the age difference but the fact that he was more like family. We would sneak around and spend time at his place. He took care of me and became someone I could depend on. He always made sure I had all I needed and every time we saw each other he would give me spending money. He made sure I could always tell him if I needed anything. Shortly after we started "dating", he declared his love for me and his intentions to marry me but I was only 17, he was 34. My grandma noticed that each time I was with him, I returned home with money and it wasn't long before she would ask me when would I see him next? I love my grandma; however, she was somewhat materialistic. She seemed to care little about what I was doing as long as I came home with money.

About a year later, I had the appointment at the American Consulate for my green card interview. By then, my sisters had joined me in Colombia as we completed the long process of becoming legal residents of the US. Now,

I could go back to New York if I chose to! However, I was having a great time in Colombia and did not want to return to the US.

I had previously told my older boyfriend how unhappy I was living with my grandma. Without hesitation, he helped me rent an apartment and I moved out, my twin joined me. We had little furniture but that did not bother us, I was elated to be on my own; accountable to no one. Although I was used to going as I pleased, I was on my own. My relationship with this man was about to end. It was a great run but since my mom was not happy with me; she didn't give me much choice. So, I decided to return to New York.

"Don't be fooled by those who speak their empty words and deceptive teachings telling you otherwise"
Ephesians 5:6

I looked forward to getting back with my boyfriend T. My goodness, while I was in Colombia, I went from one relationship to the next, trying to fill a void I didn't know I had. This desire to feel less empty inside led me to spend time with one man after another. Following my arrival back to New York, my mom helped me find a job at the company she'd been working at for years. I was excited to make my own money and not have to depend on anyone for my needs. I had grown used to being independent for the past year and a half while living in Colombia and was not about to start relying on my mom for money. My first day at work was like any first day at a new job: quick orientation and filling out some paperwork. I was paired with a young man named Hugo to show me the ropes; he was really nice but a bit conceited and a flirt. A couple of weeks since beginning my new job, I made plans to surprise my boyfriend, T, in Queens. When I arrived, his mom said he was out with friends, but I was welcomed to make myself at home and wait for him. She also left to run errands. I couldn't wait to see him. Although I can't quite say I missed T while in

Colombia, I was looking forward to picking up where we left off. Apparently, T had also been quite busy in my absence. Poking around, I found a love letter signed by a girl named Christina around the CD Player. As I read the letter, I could tell the girl was young, quite inexperienced of whom T took advantage. Clearly, they were both involved. I got a hold of her number and called. She was actually a very sweet girl who told me that she knew who I was and T used to compare her to me. He was her first boyfriend and lover. Christina was aware that I was back in the states and T had told her that he had no intentions to go back with me. I felt the blood rushing to my face but kept my composure. Obviously, he was lying to her for we had gotten back together almost as soon as I landed. We chatted for a few more minutes and I liked her even more. I was angry that he took advantage of her, she was only 16 years old. When my boyfriend finally got home, I told him what I had discovered. He denied everything. He said he broke things off with her when I came back but I wasn't stupid; I knew he was playing games and I ended the relationship with him.

"Live in the truth and keep your promises"
Proverbs12:22

T was relentless and would not stop calling me. He begged me to give him another chance and promised that he would never cheat on me again. Eventually, I gave in and decided to get back with him. He said he had not seen Christina nor spoken with her. But I had her phone number and I called her and we talked about him. I had a feeling they were still together and her carrying on over the phone about how they loved each other confirmed my suspicions. Poor girl! She didn't even know who her supposed "lover" was. I confessed to Christina that I was calling her because T and I were getting back together and he had denied they were still involved. I was not about to let him off the hook that easy. It was time to teach him a lesson. I told Christina about my plan for the 2 of us to pay him a surprise visit at work and confront him face to face. She agreed! The night before our visit, I called to confirm that she was still onboard with my plan but she had changed her mind and wasn't going. My persuasive words, coupled with a promise to drag her out of her house by her hair probably helped. She knew of my reputation for fighting. The next day we met and she looked even younger than I expected; quite timid and very afraid. I walked into the electronics store where T worked and asked a salesman to get him. Meanwhile, Christina was waiting for us in the pizzeria next door. He was so happy to see me and with a huge smile gave me a tight squeeze. I invited him to pizza for lunch and asked him to meet me at the pizzeria when ready. In the meantime, Christina and I waited inside, facing the entrance of the place. When T came in, he saw the two of us together, his jaw dropped and for a minute he went quite pale. He looked at me then at her and said: "fine, if this is how it's going to be, then let it be. I don't need either one of you" and walked right out. Mission accomplished! He was exposed. He knew not to return with his lies ever again. Perhaps the distance and time in Colombia allowed me to realize that I didn't miss him much and that was ultimately the end of that relationship.

Meanwhile, I was truly enjoying my new job. The company where I worked manufactured circuit boards for automobiles and soon, I was moved from cleaning these boards in the back room to testing them for short-circuits in the front. I quickly excelled and became one of the highest volume producers in the department. I made new friends and during the summer months, we would go straight to the beach after our overnight shift. Before I knew it, the month of October had crept up on me and I realized one evening while at work that I had not finished my studies. It was not intentional but I was now a school dropout. It didn't seem to bother me as much for I felt I needed money more than an education. Hugo was now in charge of bringing me the circuit panels for me to test. He was very thoughtful and kind and would flirt with me every chance he got. I enjoyed his coquettish behavior but he had a girlfriend and I was not interested in getting in the middle of that relationship. I knew how it felt to be betrayed.

*"You've gone into my future to prepare the way,
and in kindness you follow behind me to spare me
from the harm of my past."*
Psalm 139:5

One day while my mom was out running errands, I packed my belongings, wrote a note and left home. I moved in with my mom's ex and my stepsisters from a few years back. I couldn't be happier! I was able to catch up on sleep during my commute to Long Island. I reconnected with my sisters – it was as if we were never apart. I carpooled into Queens with a coworker, Jose, who lived in my neighborhood. He was smitten with me and I took advantage of that. Despite his pursuits, I knew enough to not get seriously involved. I was honest with Jose from the beginning but that didn't stop him from chasing me around. He would constantly tell me that he wanted to spend time with me and I used that to my benefit. One day I borrowed his car for a joy ride– the problem with that was I did not know how to drive. I thought – *how hard can it be?* He gave me the keys to his baby. I took my step sisters along for the ride with not a care in the world. I was about to make a left onto a busy intersection and saw a car fast approaching. I did not even make an attempt to get out of the way; to stop or even slow down when the car hit us! I panicked not from the impact but because my sisters were screaming in fear. I kept on driving and smashed into a stop sign; I put the car on reverse and drove off hitting other cars that were parked on the street until the oldest of the sisters told me to focus and stop the car. Immediately, I was filled with regret at the sheer disregard for not only my life but also the lives of three beautiful girls, whom I adored! They trusted me enough to get in the car with me and I let them down.

"But rather, his 'delay' simply reveals his
loving patience toward you, because he does
not want any to perish but all to come to repentance."
2 Peter 3:9

Looking back, I realize that God's hand of protection was over us because we walked away unscathed returning to Jose only with the side mirror in my hand. We were overtaken by the adrenaline and I did not fully process what had just occurred. If I had, I would have cried for so many reasons: the lives I put in danger, for being cavalier with my own life, for how careless I was in totaling my friend's car, for betraying his feelings and his trust. As he saw us approaching by foot, he asked about his car. I proceeded to tell him what happened, leaving out a few details. He was most concerned with our safety and well-being. However, his car was a complete loss, he never made me feel bad about it and I didn't even offer to help pay for anything! I was like a tornado destroying everything in its path. No denying that I was spiraling out of control. *Was I that careless?* As I reflect, I can see the awareness begin. Even then there were traces of God's faithfulness in my life. Even then, He loved me, and His love would never change even if I chose not to love Him back.

Early that November Hugo surprised me with a visit to let me know that his relationship with his girlfriend was over. By then, he had found another job and we had not seen each other for a bit. We talked for a while and before he left, I agreed to go on a date.

That night I was overcome with anticipation, yet I had no idea that this man would change my life. We drove around talking for hours getting to know each other; I was intrigued. My mother and my sisters urged me to be careful; obviously they were not happy for me. I knew in my heart that one of the reasons why they didn't particularly care for this guy was because of Jose. My mom warned me that Jose was a good guy and apparently Hugo was not.

That Thanksgiving, Hugo introduced me to his family and they seemed genuine and we got along right away. His father was also Colombian, so we immediately bonded over our culture. My new boyfriend and I started spending a lot of time together and quickly our relationship turned serious. The following February I moved out completely on my own and found a basement apartment that had no windows. That suited me perfectly since after working all night I needed to go home to sleep. Coming to the darkness of my new home was ideal. My boyfriend spent a lot of time there and I enjoyed making dinner for him. I wasn't quite making ends meet; he had no idea that I struggled financially. Lucky for me I was still friends with Evelyn from middle school; she used to write the lyrics of songs for me to learn. Her husband had a produce delivery route. Evelyn knew what I was going through and her husband would drop off mangos for me. At one point that was all I had to eat and it became my breakfast, lunch and dinner. I was too proud to ask my family – however, I became aware of the kindness of my friends and I was very grateful.

"For there is nothing that is hidden that won't be disclosed, and there is no secret that won't be brought out into the light!"
Mark 4:22

This new relationship anchored me and I finally stopped chasing trouble. I turned my attention to Hugo and was finally in a stable relationship for the first time ever. One day, we were in his car and he put his hand on my lap. I was startled and froze. He noticed my reaction and I felt compelled to reveal my secret. His reaction surprised me. He was extremely upset and said he wanted to hurt my father. I could not believe that he was so upset for something that had happened to me as a child. This revelation brought us closer together and I began to fall in love with him.

In May of that year, my twin sister gave birth to my niece, Lu. Until then, I was not familiar with that love. Lu engulfed me with a foreign kind of love, and I felt it would explode out of my chest every time I saw her. This little girl immediately stole my heart. She was beautiful and I could not get enough of her. Many days after work, I would stop by to see her. All I wanted was to hold her in my arms and kiss her tiny face.

I enjoyed living alone and felt pretty proud of myself as an independent woman. It didn't matter that I could barely make ends meet and there were many days when all I had to eat was mangos. After almost a year of dating and after a break in at my place, Hugo asked me to move in with him at his parents' house. Shortly after moving in together, I missed my period, but I was afraid to take a pregnancy test. The questions overwhelmed me. *How could I be so damn stupid? What is wrong with me?? Perhaps, I'm not pregnant… it's just the stress of my new environment.* I spent a few nights playing "what if" scenarios in my head. He was still in college and working full time and for sure there was no room in his life for a child. What if he didn't want me to keep the baby? After a few days, I had to know. I told his brother and we went to buy a pregnancy test. His brother and I had become close friends. While my boyfriend was in the bedroom studying, I took the test. I was praying for a negative result. It was just a few minutes but it seemed like an eternity and all the while I was talking myself out of the what if "I am pregnant scenario." I was terrified as the line that confirmed I was pregnant appeared on the tiny screen of the pregnancy test. My heart sank yet I felt alive and when I shared the news with his brother, congratulating me, he hugged so tight I felt my ribs almost cracking. Would Hugo share the same sentiment? At that very moment, I decided to keep my baby; it did not matter if he or anyone opposed; I was determined to make it even if it was on my own. Truth is that for years I carried the burden of guilt for terminating the pregnancies. I was quietly fighting depression and anxiety. I took a deep breath and shared the pregnancy news with my boyfriend. I had been right to be concerned about his reaction; unlike his brother, Hugo was not happy. I tried to understand, he said everything I already knew. We were too young; he was in school and working full-time; where would we find time to raise a child? I looked straight at him.

"So what? I am not asking you to quit school or work. I am having this child even if you don't want me to." I was ready to walk away from him if he didn't accept the fact that I was keeping our baby.

I believe he was hoping for a false positive result because he asked me to see a doctor for a retest. The result was the same – I was pregnant. It was a rainy day, but the sun was peeking through the clouds just for me.

"A person may have many ideas concerning
God's plan for his life, but only the designs of
his purpose will succeed in the end."
Proverbs 19:21

As the days went by my excitement grew but I was also filled with fear of losing my baby. What if this turned out to be another Molar pregnancy? What if God punished me and I lost the baby; what if the baby was born sick? What if I died while giving birth? Surely, God was not happy with me; with my past and I would have to pay for all I had done. Many nights I laid in bed rubbing my belly and throughout the day I would cradle my baby bump. One day as I was waiting to be picked up for work, I was looking out the window when I felt little bubbles popping in my womb and I realized that my baby was moving. For as long as I live, I will never forget how grateful I was for another chance to be a mom.

My boyfriend and I were scared, we had no clue how to parent but we had decided to stay together and do our best to raise our child in a stable home environment. However, more often than not I doubted I would be a good mom to my unborn child. All I knew was how to fight and get in trouble; qualities not exactly that of a good mother, I still felt broken.

Hugo and I sublet the apartment where his grandparents used to live in Astoria, Queens. It was a 2-bedroom apartment and the perfect size for our growing family. I continued to commute to Long Island for work but had already decided to not return after our child was born; I didn't want to be that far from our baby. When folks at work would ask me the gender of the child, they were surprised that I chose not to know. I never cared for surprises, but life had truly given us this surprise and was guaranteed to be beautiful. I also quietly feared the idea of having a boy. I just couldn't handle the thought. The experiences I had with that gender, especially my dad, made me sick. What if he grew up to be like my dad, and he abused his daughters? Or what if he was cruel to his sons like my dad was to my brother Carlos? But no one needed to know of those fears.

I had a lovely intimate baby shower at my boyfriend's parents' house. The next day, as I was putting away the gifts, I would bring the tiny clothes to my nose, deeply inhaling the fragrance of the fabric softener. A couple more weeks and the baby would arrive! The baby room was decorated in neutral colors and Hugo and I picked out names but would make the decision when the time came.

My older sister and I were pregnant at the same time. When she gave birth, I went to see her at the hospital and that same night at around one in the morning, contractions began. In this time of desperation, I only thought of my mom so I called her – she calmed me down and told me to wait until my contractions were five minutes apart. She reassured me that the pain I was feeling was normal and that I would be okay. As we hung up the phone, she reminded me that soon I would be holding this baby I had waited nine months to meet. For the next five hours, I watched TV and timed my contractions. I had heard horror stories of women in labor but nothing had prepared me for this. The pain was crippling as the contractions continued to intensify. Finally, when I couldn't take it, I asked Hugo to take me to the hospital but I was quickly sent back home – although I was ready – the baby was not. On our second trip to the hospital – although I felt my uterus being pulled like a rope in a tug of war – the doctors suggested I walk in the lobby while waiting for the contractions lasting longer than a minute… I wanted to be put out of this misery. I felt like giving up – I was in agony. Despite the pain, I stayed true to my plan of not getting the epidural. Finally 17 hours after I felt my first contraction – we finally met. Samantha was born at 6:42pm – May 18, 1994.

She had a head full of black thick hair and eyes so big the moon in all its fullness could not be compared to. God had had compassion on me and listened to my fears and gave me a little girl. Initially, I did not think she was the most beautiful baby; obviously the trauma of birth. Once they brought her back all cleaned – she was the most beautiful and delicate baby. I felt my fears dissipate and I loved her with a love that was bigger than life. I did not want to part from her even if it was just for a little while; I wanted her all for myself.

When I was discharged from the hospital, I rode in the back of the car and my eyes did not move away from my little girl. It was just the two of us – nothing else existed. I held her tiny hand the entire time in awe of her and in disbelief that she was my daughter. A few hours later, I felt like everything was falling apart and our first day home with her was a disaster! I couldn't get her to stop crying. I checked her diaper and she was dry; she had slept most of the day, yet she was crying, and I was at a loss for what to do. Wouldn't my maternal instinct kick in and I would know what to do? I decided to call my mom and sobbing I told her

I was clueless about what to do and how to help my baby girl. She asked when was the last time I fed her? I realized then that she was hungry! After feeding, she fell asleep and I lost it. I was brokenhearted and I sobbed thinking I didn't know how to care for her – I was the worst mom in the world and I had just gotten started. How could I not know that my baby girl was hungry? Certainly, I would also fail at this.

As time went by, I began to feel more and more depressed. I had not heard the term postpartum depression, so I attributed my feelings to my past – because it was what I knew made me depressed. I became extremely irritable and even violent towards my live-in boyfriend and the father of my child. Anything would set me off, the magnitude was such that I became physically abusive towards him. Afterwards, the guilt would set in and I would become more depressed; it was a vicious cycle. I couldn't stand myself, I would stand in front of the bathroom mirror, crying, feeling worthless. I hated looking at my reflection yet couldn't look away because I had to find ways to torment myself.

Chapter Eleven

MARRIED LIFE

About four months after my daughter's birth, her dad and I were married. They say every girl often dreams of her wedding day but that was not me. Not sure why but I just didn't. My boyfriend and I were already living together so the wedding was just a formality. Our baby girl was going to be baptized; she already had her dad's last name; not to feel left out, I told Hugo I wanted to have his last name as well.

There wasn't a one bended knee proposal, nor a ring. It was just a conversation as I ironed clothes. I wanted to feel like I belonged to a family. My desire was that the three of us share the same name especially when I filled out forms. So, we tied the knot! We bought our rings at a discounted jeweler. The rings were very thin, and the stone was almost microscopic but that didn't matter. I've never been materialistic so to me, the rings were perfect! Besides accommodating folks' schedule, we finally set a wedding date. We really wanted everyone to be there. My mom and I went shopping for a dress, but it was a courthouse wedding so instead of a fancy dress I opted for a black skirt and white jacket. Our parents, immediate family and a couple friends of mine were invited. My friend Evelyn asked about a reception? a cake? The answer was a no and no. Her loving gesture was to show up with a cake. The Happy Birthday was smeared off to read Happy Wedding; it clearly was a cake for a girl with bright pink ruffles. Nothing like a last-minute display of love; oh, how she treasured our friendship.

Following our brief wedding adventure, we jumped into the life as full-time parents. Our daughter was very smart. She took her first steps and was completely potty-trained before her first birthday. I was so proud of her but also proud of myself – for my dedication to teach her so many skills. I cherished her. She was my only time of true happiness!! Apart from her, I was miserable. No one knew me; the true me. On the outside, I was smiling but secretly on the inside I was in such pain and weeping. I would visit my mom and sisters and spend time with my two nieces and my little brother; those moments were some of the few that I felt happiness. The sad reality was that there was no true happiness; I lived in a dark tunnel. I was in an emotional prison; my legs were bound by invisible shackles and I had to muster all my strength just to move. Over the first year of my daughter's life, I was working in Manhattan at a small medical company. I enjoyed my work and the social interaction but I missed my little one, she had changed my life and was the reason for my smile. However, there were moments when I still grappled with my past. I was happy being a married woman with a new name. I was no longer identified with the name of the one who dishonored me. I was the mom to an amazing little girl who was extremely smart but there were moments when I wondered about the babies whose pregnancies I terminated. I couldn't find complete happiness. I was still tormented by my past.

As our first wedding anniversary was approaching, I decided to do something special for my husband. He had endured so much from me. I loved him and tried to be a good wife, but we were far from perfect. I was excited to plan a surprise getaway. I didn't make much money but after a couple of phone calls, I booked a weekend getaway to a resort in the Pocono Mountains in Pennsylvania. It didn't cost much; all we had to do was sit through a presentation and they would cover lodging and a meal. I was thrilled! I had everything taken care of and it would be an amazing weekend for just the two of us. I was looking forward to some rest and relaxation. I struggled to contain my excitement about this trip for several weeks until the day finally arrived. As I waited for my husband to pick me up at work, I daydreamed about what our weekend would be like. I couldn't wait to see his face when I would tell him about my plan; I knew for sure it would be a memorable next two days. His parents were watching our daughter, so we had peace of mind and could enjoy ourselves. The sky was gray, and it had been drizzling all day but there was nothing that would dampen my mood about our trip. As I had been anticipating, my husband was touched and very surprised when he heard about my plan for our anniversary. I couldn't wipe the smile off my face, in that moment, I was happy. I found myself looking out the window in gratitude. I took a big breath and thanked God for all I had. I was a 21-year-old young woman, a mom, and was married to the love of my life. I truly felt blessed.

After driving a couple of hours, we pulled in. The resort was impressive. Since it was late, we grabbed something to eat and went back to our room to soak in the heart shaped Jacuzzi. Our plan was to relax for the night and go exploring the next day. In the morning, after breakfast, we walked around the resort and went for a swim in the indoor pool. We spent the day enjoying each other's company; dreaming about our future together and wondering how we would celebrate many more anniversaries. We wrapped up the night by celebrating our anniversary with dinner, drinking and dancing. We danced nonstop and by the time we were ready to go back to our room, I was exhausted and had a little too much to drink. Walking back, we began to tease each other. At first, we were being playful and our senses were in overdrive. Perhaps it was a combination of our passion and the drinks, but we were feeling very frisky, and allowed our imagination to go wild. What started as innocent role play morphed into something bigger than the two of us. That night I walked through the door of a hidden secret. I allowed my physical being to engage in my husband's new world and I had no notion of how it began, how to be part of it nor how far it would go. I became a participant of someone's waging war of reality vs fantasy. That night defined our new journey within the confines of our bedroom.

After that anniversary weekend, my husband and I no longer made love to each other. I participated in exploits that would defile our bed. I know I could have said no the very first time; I could have had taken back my power and my peace but, in that instance, I became that little girl who had no voice and who was there to please. I did not know who my creator was and who I was truly destined to be. For the remainder of my marriage, I blamed myself for not speaking up, for being a "willing participant." I was on a downward spiral of my own demise. It was not an isolated incident. It happened again. We role played people we knew; it was his way of inviting "others" into our bedroom. Our intimacy became so unhealthy that we could no longer simply be together loving each other, appreciating who we were in our relationship.

Chapter Twelve

A MARRIAGE BROKEN

"The eye is the lamp of the body. So, if your eye is healthy, your whole body will be full of light, but if your eye is bad, your whole body will be full of darkness. If then the light in you is darkness, how great is the darkness!"
Matthew 6: 22-23

Watching pornography before intimacy became our new ritual. My husband would compare me with the porn actress on the screen and others not on the screen. The language he used mimicked the profanity that came out of the actors. We became performers in our own home. What began as curiosity, became occasional and before we knew it, had become our new normal. Yet another secret to carry. Outside of awful confinement, everything seemed typical. I still enjoyed going to work and being a mom and of course, I enjoyed being his wife. I wanted to support my husband who was in the process of becoming a correctional officer hoping to join the police force after that. The benefits would be great for our family. Everything pointed towards a great secure future. No one except my husband and I knew of our perverted secret.

Despite the cracks in our marriage, I loved the sense of having my own family but being a mom was what ultimately tamed me. However, I was still capable of losing my composure in a millisecond. Any argument would quickly escalate to physical attacks towards my husband. Violent outbursts and the ability to hurt him was relatively common by now. He never touched me, but rather would try to help calm me down. I was like the hulk. I would turn into an angry monster, that eventually, would turn back to my normal self.

I was extremely careful to keep my daughter from witnessing these moments of fury. I did not want her to continue this cycle. My dad was the monster, but I now found myself filled with his rage, unable to contain my emotions. Funny how I became that which I hated the most. That year, my marriage lost such a vital component of a healthy marriage: the respect for each other. Without respect, the foundation of our marriage had a huge fracture, visible to only the two of us. From the outside, we had a great marriage but, on the inside, my walls were closing in and my world started to become darker and darker. The depression deepened as I contemplated ending my life. I wanted to numb the pain of many years of abuse. Our intimacy now was the trigger that caused emotions I thought I would never relive. Little by little the wound began to stench like the start of an infection. There were times when I locked myself in the bathroom and cried. I would try to envision a happy future; perhaps I could go back to school? Or perhaps we would heal and love one another without the dirty gunk. My future appeared hopeless until I thought of my little girl and then my feeling of worthlessness would go away enough for me to regain my composure and face the day. This became a pattern, a pattern that could not and would not hold up to the intense strain for much longer.

One day, while my little one was napping, Hugo and I got into a big argument that left me feeling hollow inside. I don't remember the details; I was crying quite loudly, begging for attention. I felt so low at that moment, the walls of the tunnel had completely closed in and I had had enough. I was not worth loving, nor a good role model for my child. I believed her life would be better without me. Similar to the fear I had about having a boy that might turn out like my dad, I felt my daughter would not turn out like me if I was gone. *Is this the culmination of a life of depression?* This is what the enemy would have us believe! I was completely exhausted fighting my demons. I was tired of the crying, tired of the tantrums, the self-pity, the self-hatred, the incompetency and inadequacy. I didn't want to live and decided to finally end it all. I checked on my baby and proceeded to the bathroom. I frantically removed the seal of a bottle of pain killers we had recently purchased and filled my hand with pills, lots of them. My husband asked me what I was trying to accomplish, and I answered:

"I'm done with everything. I'm done with you. I'm done with our marriage. I'm going to kill myself."

As he watched, I swallowed a hand full of pills and then filled my hand again and swallowed those too. It was horrifying to know that my husband had just watched and did nothing to stop me. In fact, he went back to the living room and sat down to continue watching TV. I laid down for a bit and waited for death to come. Suddenly, the thought of that death magnified, and I began to regret what I had done. I was consumed with the notion that my daughter would need me; I would guide her and watch her grow into a lovely woman. She WASN'T better off without me. I knew this was a life revelation that I couldn't share with my husband. At that moment I was scared. My life really didn't matter to him either. I called my twin sister who had always been there for me and in between sobs gave her details of what I had done. It was my goodbye in case I didn't make it; she was my last comfort. Soon, I felt sick; I was dizzy and the ringing in my ears was almost deafening. I closed my eyes and as I cried, I had a conversation with God. I pleaded for forgiveness and a chance to live. I cried for my daughter who would grow up without a mom, I cried for my sister who would lose her childhood best friend. I cried for myself. *How did I get to this point? Why did my life turn out this way?*

I heard a faint knock on the door and the doorbell ringing. I got to my feet and walked to the living room to find two paramedics. They were there because someone had called 911 to report an attempted suicide. Sadly, even in my agony I knew it had not been my husband. They asked me several questions, about what happened. I was open and honest. They requested the bottle of pills, so my husband brought it to them. Out of one hundred pain relievers, there were only fourteen left. I had swallowed 86 pills! What had I done? After taking my vitals, one of the paramedics determined that I had to go to the ER. Still not understanding the gravity of the situation, Hugo asked:

"Is it really necessary to take her to the hospital?"

I will never forget the look on the paramedic's face as he responded:

"Sir, if you don't want your wife to die here in your home, we need to take her to the hospital."

Maybe the paramedic said that because he was taken aback by the question or perhaps that would have been the case if I didn't go. I recall the sound of the sirens as they drove me to the hospital; I wasn't feeling well and was terrified but I was also ashamed and embarrassed. It was probably written all over my face and the paramedic in a kind tone assured me that I would be okay. He had shown me more compassion than my own husband.

At the hospital, I was recognized by an old friend who worked there. Concerned, he asked what brought me in? I was so weak that I couldn't have answered the question even if I wanted to – which I didn't. Out of nowhere, my heart began beating extremely fast; I felt as if I was drifting. Suddenly, I passed out. When I came to, I was surrounded by a group of medical professionals that explained I had gone into cardiac arrest! I don't remember feeling scared at all, in fact, I don't recall feeling anything. Once I was stabilized, I was given activated charcoal to decontaminate my stomach and prevent my organs from shutting down due to the poison I had consumed. I immediately started to vomit until my stomach was empty; my life had been spared. I knew it was something greater than the charcoal. I wasn't actually clear on who God was or how He worked, but I knew something bigger than myself had saved me from certain death. Although I was safe, I still felt sick and exhausted and closed my eyes to sleep. I woke up just enough to see that I had been moved to another room and then I drifted back to sleep.

I woke up as my husband was checking up on me. He brought a picture of our little one and at that moment I broke down crying. *How could I have been so selfish to play with my life this way?* My daughter was the most precious human being in the world. She needed me and I needed her. I asked God for forgiveness once again and thanked Him for keeping me alive. For the next couple of days, I was evaluated by a psychiatrist and it was the first time I ever talked to a professional about my struggle with depression and its root causes. It felt good to unload, to talk about how worthless and insignificant I felt my entire life. It was a relief to not be afraid; judged; nor asked *"why I didn't ever say anything?"* a question my mom asked when I was cornered into telling her how my father had sexually abused me for years.

As good as it felt to talk about what hurt me emotionally, the worst physical pain was having the nurses do an arterial blood oxygen test. Unlike a regular blood test where they draw blood from your vein, this test required that the blood be drawn from an arterial artery. It was a small price to pay for what I had tried to do – I felt I deserved it.

After multiple evaluations by the psychiatrist, I was discharged. The doctor recommended that I see a therapist to begin my healing process as well as taking an antidepressant to help me cope with my feelings. I was happy to return home to my little girl.

For the next year or so, not much changed in my life and I did not heed the advice of the doctor to follow up with therapy and start medication right away. I was glad to have the chance of watching my child grow up. She was a beauty! I knew my husband "loved me", there was no doubt in my mind; however, we did not respect our marriage. Our love for one another was extremely unhealthy. We did not have God and we didn't honor our vows as we continued to defile our intimacy. Our imagination was wild, our thoughts filthy and our hearts uncleaned, therefore out of our mouths we spoke vulgar words. When my little girl was 3 years old, her dad was finally in the police academy having made the transition from corrections officer. Soon after, we decided to get pregnant again. We loved being parents and enjoyed every minute with our daughter. From playing outside at the park, running through the sprinklers – just watching her grow right before our eyes to even the moments when she kept us up at night because she had fallen ill. I felt a sense of pride that she was mine as we watched movies together in her room, and she would start belting out the songs coming out from the screen.

We thought that it would take a while to get pregnant, it didn't. While at I work, I realized my period was late and bought a pregnancy test. I followed the instructions, and in a few minutes, that felt like years, the results indicated that I was pregnant. I could hardly contain myself. I was pregnant! I remember this day vividly. I was on cloud nine and wanted to open a window and yell it out for the world to hear. I'm going to be a mom again! I called my twin and told her she was going to be a Titi again. On my way home, I stopped at the store and picked up a card for my husband along with some chocolate and I could not wait to give him the good news.

Chapter Thirteen

BITTERSWEET

"Every good and perfect gift is from above,
coming down from the Father of the heavenly lights,
who does not change like shifting shadows."
James 1:17

I was so excited to tell Hugo we were expecting. I left the card and chocolate on the table and next to it, the pregnancy test and went to bed. I waited anxiously for him to get home. My heart was beating fast and I couldn't keep from smiling. I heard the door open when my husband arrived. All of the sudden I became aware of every noise as he walked over to the table, picked up the card and read it and next thing I heard was a huge "WHAT?!!!" My husband's reaction to this news was better than I expected. I came out of the bedroom and we hugged tightly and for the first time in two years I felt close to my husband again.

This pregnancy was different. I did not gain much weight, and I began to experience contractions early-in my seventh month. Despite the difference, I loved every minute of my pregnancy. My little girl was so happy to be a big sister, she would rub and kiss my belly all the time. Much like the previous pregnancy, I was not curious to find out the gender of my unborn child. One day, while we were sitting in bed watching one her favorite TV shows, I asked,

"Do you want to have a baby brother or baby sister?"
She answered without hesitation.
"A sister!" Secretly, I was hoping the same.
On the morning of April 17, 1998, I awoke with cramps and intense pressure in my abdomen. I was in labor, and I

knew the birth would be soon. My baby urgently wanted to make an entrance! As I arrived at the hospital, the staff rushed me to the delivery room. The nurse quickly broke my water and within minutes, my little girl's wish came true, and my second baby girl, Ariel, was born. Our family of four was now complete. The moment I laid eyes on her I knew she was very special. I looked her over as moms usually do, she was beautiful and perfect. I was relieved to have another girl; even more relieved that my husband and I decided not to have any more children. Samantha had already taught me how to be a mom; how to love selflessly. Because of her, I learned I could give more than I thought capable. This time around I was more relaxed and didn't worry about every little thing. My heart was full and content with my two daughters and that was alright for me.

Not long after I gave birth to Ariel, Hugo and I resumed our fantasies. What had started as simple imaginations was seeping into our actual lives. The door we had walked through on our first anniversary had led us to a lifestyle that I had never dreamed of living. I came to this realization one day as my husband and I returned from a trip. We had traveled to Six Flags in New Jersey with some friends. As we returned to New York, we carpooled with one of my husband's co-workers. The ride back was filled with flirtatious words and looks. I felt tingling all over my body realizing the chemistry between his friend and I. Although nothing happened, I was appalled that I had these feelings – and that I thought they were normal.

A few months later, we decided to move into a larger house in a nicer neighborhood. This would be a new season for us as a family. Looking back, I am still horrified at who I was. I had zero moral values. I was a sheep alone with no sheperd; I really had lost my way. I had no boundaries with myself nor with my husband. My marriage was falling apart. We went from fantasizing to making suggestions and encouraging extramarital affairs.

I had my first affair with his friend, the one from Six Flags. Oddly enough I did not tell my husband; not because I was afraid of the outcome; I was afraid that he would use the details to engage in the world of his perversion.

It was at this time that I began to see a therapist who helped me begin to confront my past and made a huge impression in my life. Until this day, I warmly think of him. I also had a new job that I really enjoyed. My coworkers were lovely and I used my 45-minute commute to the city to read. Despite my failing marriage, I loved my husband. Not easy to understand, especially since I was unfaithful, though I had no doubt that I loved him but I had no boundaries; no lines that I would not cross. I remember that I used to cry a lot during this season of my life. I yearned to be wanted. I longed to be the "only one" not just someone who was shared with ghosts. I was in love despite how much I hated being compared and objectified. I was very confused. My daughters were my strength. God used my daughters to provide strength despite my unawareness of Him. At the time – He was my strength.

My husband became distant, I attributed it to his high stress job. I did not push to know anything else either. One night as we were in bed and began talking about our lives together, I asked questions for which I was unprepared to hear the answers. My husband confessed that he did not love me, and it would be best to go our separate ways. I sat up and could not stop my tears. I wanted to be strong and not cry but that was impossible. This man, no matter how flawed and manipulative, was my world. As deeply as I was hurt, I stopped myself short of begging him to reconsider because in the end, I knew it was better if he left.

He moved back with his parents until he could find a place. I was hurting and I would lay in bed wondering how long would I feel such pain? My deepest desire was for my husband to come back and take me in his arms; to be so close I could smell his breath. I prayed that it would be as when we were first married. *Why did he fall out of love?*

Was I not good enough? All I wanted was to be loved. On Valentine's Day 1999, I wrote him a letter. I had asked him to come back; telling him how much I missed him and that no one could love him the way "I knew how to." But I never gave him the letter. I was consumed with the idea that I was defined by how wild I was; defined by my polluted thoughts. Where did it get me? The months that followed were extremely hard for me. The girls were too young to notice anything was amiss. I wrote many more letters to him. I poured my heart out. My feelings suspected there might be someone else, but I could not bring myself to ask him. I loved my husband in my own way, I wanted to fight for us but feared the rejection. My thoughts consumed me – I played all scenarios of getting back together but knew it was all in vain. My indiscretion brought about such deep guilt.

Three months later, we were back together; I could not have been happier. Despite the feeling that something was still wrong, I chose to focus on my happiness. This time the ghost had a name and was real. I would have walked away, had I known how much more it would hurt to be back together. I became extremely insecure as a woman and a wife. I felt so minimized, but again, because I was afraid that he would leave – I did not confront him. I thought I would be happy that he was back but instead I felt sad and afraid because in my heart I knew we would not last. As the days turned into weeks and weeks into months, I started to feel complacent. One night during dinner, I looked around the table and took a mental note of my feelings. Because I was a mother, this was a wonderful time in my life, and I was over the moon, though cautious. I knew that happiness would be short lived. Subconsciously, I waited for the hurricane to come to destroy everything in its path.

The next couple of years seemed great. I continued to see my therapist and take my medication though I felt like I no longer needed it. I was cautiously happy. Our daughters were the center of our lives and we kept busy. However, my feelings did not betray me, I was right to be cautious. That good season did not last.

A friend had called; she was in fear for her life as her husband was abusive towards her. I could hardly understand her in between sobs. She had no place to go; I invited her to stay with us for the night. Sadly, she had to leave without her children because her husband would not allow them to leave the house. The next day as she was ready to get her children, her husband threatened her so she stayed with us for a couple of days until she could plan how to get her little ones back. One night, Hugo, my friend and I sat to watch TV after my girls went to bed. I felt a familiar unsettling feeling but shrugged it off since all seemed well between us; plus, it was nice to have another female friend to talk to. The next day my friend called me at work to tell me that she was leaving the house right away. At first, she refused to tell me why but, after some urging, she mentioned that Hugo had made advances toward her. He had come home drunk after a baseball game and asked her to lie in bed with him. I then understood why she wanted to leave immediately while he was still asleep, and I could not stop her.

When confronted, not only did he deny it; he even accused my friend of being the one who came on to him. I knew better and became furious that he even suggested such a thing. She was not like us. She was a woman with boundaries; unlike me. I discussed the events that transpired with my therapist and at his suggestion I asked for space until I cooled off and was ready to have a civilized conversation with my husband. I was hurting and I had started to drink and self-medicate in high doses. I wasn't trying to hurt myself – but somehow wanted the pain in my heart to go away. At my therapist's prompting, I admitted myself to the hospital and spent the next few days in a psychiatric ward. In a way I felt relieved to go; I was devastated. I hated myself for being blind and allowing me to be hopeful. I hated the mere thought that I was worthy to be happy. I felt so wounded. My husband still did not admit he was wrong and continued to shift the blame on my good friend. Although I met with a doctor daily and did group therapy, I was still numb inside. Before I was discharged, the therapist and I met with Hugo, who finally admitted it was he who came on to my friend. On our way home, I no longer wanted to discuss what had happened. Something had completely shifted inside.

Chapter Fourteen

TEMPORARY SOLUTIONS

"Woe to those who call evil good and good evil,
who put darkness for light and light for darkness,
who put bitter for sweet and sweet for bitter!"
Isaiah 5:20

After that incident, I found myself back in the dark tunnel of thoughts from which I could not seem to escape. That natural place – except this time, I understood where that would lead. The person who could care less about lines and boundaries no longer existed. No doubt I felt like a hypocrite; I felt hurt and realized that my marriage was a sham. Too many secrets to carry and yet I wasn't done. After a few more affairs, I started to feel less guilty about my indiscretions. I was doing what was expected of me. After all, Hugo encouraged me to go out and "have fun." Despite the deep feelings of remorse when I saw my daughters, my behavior continued. Self-validation eclipsed that feeling of remorse. Interesting how God had begun the change in my life through motherhood. I understood the immense love toward my daughters and their unconditional love for me! With this understanding – I reflected on how I ended those previous pregnancies. But motherhood was the only pure, untainted part of my life that had meaning. Outside of that–there was a piece missing. I was torn – was I worthy to be loved by my husband or by any other man? That part of my life was still a mess.

In the middle of the chaos we called our marriage, we decided to buy a house. I think we both silently thought that moving to a new home would change things for the better. There was certainly an excitement about being homeowners. The girls could finally make all the noise they wanted. We could have barbecues and fill the yard with our relatives and friends. In order to save enough money for a down payment, we moved in with my in-laws. We paid off our debt and, in less than a year, we were looking at properties. We settled in the suburbs outside of the city but close enough to visit our relatives within an hour. Our new home was absolutely perfect. It was a three bedroom one bath single family home just outside of the city. It was always a touching sight to watch my girls jumping and running around the house without fear of annoying our downstairs neighbors. This house became the best home for our girls where we created so many wonderful memories. My girls and I used to play house and school all the time. One day, as we were playing in our living room, I asked them a question: "Girls, how come when we play house you always choose me to play the mom?" Samantha responded with a smile and a hug and said, "Because you're the best mommy in the world!" Her younger sister, Ariel, quickly nodded her agreement. My heart was full. In that moment, I felt as if my life finally had meaning and direction.

Our family and friends loved our new house as well. And why wouldn't they? In the summer, we bought a big inflatable pool for the kids and grilled steaks and burgers on our back patio, and we were only 15 minutes from the beach! My girls quickly made friends with the neighborhood kids, and I enjoyed watching them play across the street outside of our window. In those moments I could not believe how good life appeared to be. Unfortunately, in what had become commonplace, that feeling was not meant to last. As the summer wound down, so did my excitement with life. Our mornings of playing house were replaced with rushing my girls to the school bus. From the outside, my life looked great, but the reality was that the cracks in my marriage and in my life were widening. As we settled into the new school routine, we now had time to think about our relationship and how unhappy we both were. We continued to feed off each other's pain.

"⁶For the mind-set of the flesh is death,
but the mind-set controlled by the Spirit
finds life and peace."
Romans 8:6

My marriage was very toxic. I was encouraged to cheat as long as I shared the details of my encounters. God knows how many times I lied throughout the years to satisfy his intrigue. I felt so degraded and cheap. I was conditioned to believe that I was required to do "what would make me happy" even if it did not and I knew it was wrong. Between all the cheating, indiscretions, and affairs, our marriage became extremely fragile and dishonest. It was during this time that I met a man who also embraced this lifestyle. He was fresh and exciting to me so I grew close to him, even though I knew it would only end in more heartbreak and shame. Ultimately, my husband and I became estranged again and hardly talked to each other – he had work and I had my girls. I was living a double life. I was both the devoted, fearless mom and the unfaithful emotionally drained wife who had given up on her marriage but couldn't walk away.

Deep down, despite my behavior, I wanted to stay married. During one of my sessions, my therapist suggested that my husband come inside for the last 20 minutes. We talked as we had in the past and told the therapist that we wanted our marriage to work. The therapist gave us "homework" and asked my husband to commit to joining the sessions regularly until we were in a better place. I recall our drive back home; I was optimistic and looking forward to the exercises we had been given. Sadly, nothing changed. In fact, my husband never went back to therapy with me. I was disappointed and annoyed that I allowed myself to believe that there was anything left in my marriage. That night, I wrote a letter to my dad condemning him for his actions and abuse toward me. I expressed how I was still experiencing the effects of what he had done and how that had ruined who I was. The letter, though never intended to be mailed, helped me confront my past by holding my dad accountable for his disgraceful behavior toward me for many years.

I continued the friendship with my charming guy friend. Throughout that year, he was my escape when I needed to feel wanted. There was an emptiness to be filled – which was the beginnings of a search. I didn't yet understand that my creator was in search of me. Hugo and I were living parallel lives – I would go out with my sister and our friends either locally dancing or weekend trips to South Beach, while my husband lived his own life. He was only curious if I had "misbehaved." I spent a lot of time thinking about my unhappiness. I would write Hugo letters; some I shared with him and others I kept only in my journal. I was living life on a rollercoaster of emotions.

We kept on testing the boundaries of our marriage. If it got boring or felt stale – that was our gauge to take it to the next level. We frequented places that were geared toward couples experiencing an alternative "lifestyle." Some of these places were "offsite" while others were not so subdued but still these places were repulsive and immoral; yet there we were. We visited these clubs a few times but I was getting tired of playing pretend. Pretending that I enjoyed watching and being watched. I felt dirty, disgusted with myself. I was fighting many demons, but I didn't have any armor to protect against them. Back then, I was not aware of my inner battle, but something began to shift. I felt the surroundings of perversion; that behavior that was not a bit gratifying; it would leave me feeling like trash. I immediately regretted everything about it. I began to self-assess enough to realize the causes of my low self-esteem. For the first time I was disengaging – I was struggling being there, I was no longer drifting – my senses were not allowing me to detach – I was too aware of myself – I was so unhappy that I allowed myself to be there.

Meanwhile outside of the home, I continued to build my life. I excelled as an office manager of a cardiology practice. My boss was so grateful for my work that he offered to pay my expensive monthly train fare. I graciously accepted. He was also flexible with my work hours. When my husband's work schedule changed, requiring me to be home earlier, I thought I would have to quit but I was able to adjust my schedule at work to accommodate it. I felt so appreciated at work.

One day on my commute to Manhattan from Long Island, I met a younger man. We became friends and over the course of many months that friendship turned into romance. For the first time in a long time, I felt "selfishly" cared for. I used the word selfishly in context because my new friend could not bear the thought of sharing me with anyone. That was my initial attraction to him. He was definitely a gorgeous man but that wasn't what I cared about. When we were together, he always made sure I was a priority. That was something I had never felt before.

Still feeling a sense of commitment, I decided to disclose everything to my husband. He did not take it well at all. He was furious. He couldn't believe that I had the audacity to allow another man to be kind; to look at me and appreciate all my good qualities. A few months later, my "friend" declared he had fallen for me and asked me to consider our future together. I told him I would consider, but I couldn't go with him. Silently, I desperately wanted to be with him. I was tired of the sneaking around and wanted peace. I used to think that peace was based on my circumstances. For example, if things were well, then I had peace; otherwise, I was restless. During this time, my husband and I had split yet again. This time, I moved out with the girls to a nearby house and we started to make it our new home. However, Hugo and I always found our way back to each other, like magnets. I was a sucker for punishment. Although I moved out to make a life for myself and my daughters, Hugo constantly ended up at my place. The invisible thread tied around me was still not broken. I was happy in my new house but didn't know how to retain such happiness.

Chapter Fifteen

SUMMER VACATIONS

*"The integrity of the upright guides them,
but the crookedness of the treacherous destroys them."
Proverbs 11:3*

That summer, my husband took our daughters to Florida with his family. I also took a trip of my own with my new friend. I should have been really happy during this trip, but I wasn't. I loved Puerto Rico but despite the many excursions and great food, I was unable to enjoy the trip. I couldn't shake the feeling of guilt for breaking up and separating my family. This trip allowed me to see behaviors in my "friend" that at first were endearing but now put me on edge.

I cried thinking of my girls. One day, at Flamenco Beach, I was lying in the sand trying to enjoy the beautiful nature around me but I could hardly focus on my surroundings. My mind kept on drifting to my daughters. *What were they doing? Did they understand what was really going on? Did I?* I looked out at the crystal-clear waves splashing on the shore in front of me as more and more questions flooded my mind. *Was leaving my husband the right choice? How was this going to impact my daughters in the future? How would this impact me in the future?* After our separate trips, Hugo and I took the girls to Hershey Amusement Park in Pennsylvania. We indulged on junk food and were excited to try all the roller coasters and rides. The trip was mainly planned for my daughters. We wanted them to have an enjoyable summer and create beautiful memories together. Seeing my husband interacting with our daughters reminded me of that stable life I wanted to provide for them. Despite the pain and struggle of our marriage, I wanted to give us one more shot at fixing things.

I couldn't hide from the reality: we did not love each other with the typical kind of love. The selfless, patient, caring kind of love. My husband and I had been together since I was eighteen years old so you could say that he was my constant as an adult. I cannot explain my mentality back then. I knew in my heart that we brought the very worst out of each other yet I couldn't completely detach from him. Even after I moved out, he would stop by to see me and I would submit myself to him. It truly was a vicious cycle that I wanted to break.

Following our Hershey trip, we did get back together. Not an easy decision but I was ready to give my marriage one more chance at life. My husband was very excited for us and promised that it would be different. He also gave me a beautiful wedding band. I was able to replace the almost paper-thin wedding band we had originally purchased. I quit my job in the city. I blamed the long commute for this decision, but perhaps it was more to avoid the man who had shown me "selfless love." I said goodbye to my amazing job. My boss was greatly saddened to lose his best employee but bid me farewell and wished me the best. As a farewell gift, he gave me an extra two weeks' pay on my last paycheck. Even more surprising, a few weeks later when I visited his office, he gave me a check that amounted to five times my former salary! He mentioned that he had to hire two employees to replace me and wanted me to know how much I had meant to him and the office. Wow! I didn't know it at the time but this was one of the first exhibits of God's favor in my life and it was before I even really knew Him.

The next few months were great. I found a job in a hospital on Long Island working in the Division of Plastic and Reconstructive Surgery. About three months after I started, my supervisor, impressed with my work ethic asked if I could help the division's supervisor as she was going through health issues. I was happy and honored that I would be asked to contribute in a bigger capacity but sad about the circumstances.

One day I got a call at work from my husband. My oldest daughter had been in a minor accident. I am not sure how I arrived at the hospital, but I broke down hysterically crying as I saw my little one lying in bed with a busted lip still stained by dried blood and a broken arm. Apparently, a reckless driver was going too fast and my daughter in her panic fell off her bike. I thanked God as she underwent surgery the next day and thankfully she was home two days later. The following week, she was a beauty queen for Halloween. The swollen lip had gone down, though she was wearing a cast. Nothing deterred her from going trick or treating and filling her bag with candy.

Chapter Sixteen

THE FINAL STRAW

"…and they have been adequately trained by what they've experienced to emerge with understanding of the difference between what is truly excellent and what is evil and harmful."
Hebrews 5:14

My marriage seemed to be headed in the right direction. My husband and I were communicating better and were spending more time together as well. Finally, I thought, my marriage was going to make it. During this time, I spent all my attention on being a good wife and a great mom. My job at the hospital was rewarding and I made great friends. One woman in particular, Elzie, became my best friend and closest confidant. We used to talk about everything, especially our marriages. We trusted and supported one another. She definitely helped me make it through this season of life.

During this short season, I experienced moments of happiness – but not the fullness of a happy life – if there is such a thing. Hugo and I were getting along and were enjoying each other's company. At least I thought I was. Unfortunately, all of that soon changed. Just as before, my husband and I returned to our old ways. I was torn inside because my definition of happiness may have seemed sort of twisted, but I learned to cope with the things that made me less "happy." On more than a few occasions when we were intimate, tears streamed down my face. My life was beyond crazed. I was looking for a fresh start.

I was still in search of something to fill the void. This time, it wasn't a house or a vacation, I decided to quit my job and start a new career. My new job was as an account executive at a mortgage company. I thought it would be exciting and distract me from my problems. That was but another façade that would come crumbling down when a colleague and I went to visit a broker on a sales call together. Afterward, as we were parked recapping the meeting, I could see him fondling himself from the corner of my eye. My heart sank in horror, and I completely froze. He must've sensed my discomposure; he drove me back to pick up my car. I cried so much on my way home. I became so angry at him but mostly at myself. *Why did I freeze and not say anything?* I turned into that helpless little girl who was defenseless. My coworker and I never spoke of the incident, but I made sure never to be alone in a car or anywhere else with him.

"…he had compassion for them, because they were harassed and helpless, like sheep without a shepherd."
Matthew 9:36

Despite this horrible event, this job ended up pushing me closer to God. While working there, I met two people that made a difference in my life. The first was a broker. He was an older man who loved to share his faith in God. The first day I met him, rather than talk about business, he shared about God and His love. This piqued my curiosity which was further stoked by a young lady I met a few weeks later. When I met this younger woman, Deidra, I was amazed. She had such passion for life and a beautiful smile made her even more attractive. We lived just a few minutes away from each other, so we started to spend time together. One day, Deidra told me of her Christian faith. She told me that God was her friend; someone she talked to without fear of judgement. She'd beamed whenever she talked about Him and displayed such joy when she mentioned His name. I was curious about what she had to say so I listened but didn't ask many questions. One afternoon we met up and we walked into a shop where they sold religious items. Deidra grabbed a Bible. After she paid for it, she gave it to me. I was excited about my new gift and she knew it. When I got home, I opened up the Bible and read Psalm 23; it wasn't a long chapter and was easy to memorize. I kept the Bible on my nightstand and read the Psalms. I used my yellow highlighter to go over the verses that spoke to me. I was beginning to find the Word comforting. I didn't know the background stories behind the Scripture, and I didn't need to. I found peace and hope whenever I read this Book.

"May the Lord move your hearts into a greater understanding Of God's pure love for you."
2 Thessalonians 3:5

I had reached a turning point with my job when I wasn't able to get any deals closed. I wasn't contributing much to the household bills. My husband never put pressure on me about finances, in fact, he was very good at paying bills and provided all we needed. One day, I got home very stressed out. I was out all-day visiting broker after broker but no deal was in sight. I walked into my bedroom and stood in front of my mirror and sobbed. As I felt the lowest ever, I sensed my youngest daughter, Ariel, come near and ask:

"What's wrong, Mamacita?"

Between my tears I told her why I was sad, and she took my hands and placed them on her shoulders as she reached up toward mine and prayed for me. Out of nowhere she said:

"God, won't you please help my mommy so that she is not stressed out?"

I lost it and started crying even more. My eight-year-old had seen me at a low point, stressed out and came to rescue me in prayer. At that moment, I felt not only a sense of peace and gratitude but also bewilderment. Shortly after that, I decided to return to work at the hospital. However, this time I returned as the Executive Assistant to the Chief of the Cardiothoracic Surgery Division. Again I was highly favored yet I didn't know it. Everyone was cheerful to see me back.

"Protect me from harm;
keep an eye on me like you would a child
reflected in the twinkling of your eye.
Yes, hide me within the shelter of your embrace,
under your outstretched wings."
Psalm 17:8

Along with the Bible, Deidra had also given me a bookmark with a prayer of protection written on it. Since then, each day when I got in my car to go to work, I would recite that prayer. One morning as I performed this new ritual, I reached the first red light and realized that I was still praying. The words out of my lips were just flowing. I shrugged it off and put the radio on and proceeded to pick up my daily breakfast from the deli. After picking up my breakfast sandwich and in my car, I immediately started to pray again for protection and again it flowed right out of me. My prayers were heard and answered! As I pulled out of the parking lot, I was hit full force by a dump truck. The impact was such that I ended facing the opposite direction. The trucker had not seen me. After hitting my car, the driver crashed into a utility pole bringing it down to the ground. My airbags deployed; there was glass everywhere. The ringing inside my ears was very loud; I was in shock, but I felt fine. People coming to my aid advised me to stay still; help was on the way. When the ambulance arrived, they did an initial assessment and then transported me to the Emergency Room. I told them that I was feeling okay but for precaution I had to go with them. Changing into a hospital gown, I overhead a paramedic saying I was very lucky. The severe damage of the car and the pole laying on the street was an indication of the incredible impact of the crash. It made sense that for some strange reason I had been involuntarily praying. I understood that God had been watching and it was a beautiful feeling.

"Don't let anyone disqualify you from your prize!

Don't let their pretended sincerity fool
you as they deliberately lead you"
Colossians 2:18

On Valentine's day my husband gave me a home-made card. It was a drawing of the two of us laying down by a pool with a romantic message; he appeared sincere. I do believe that he loved me just like I loved him but it was all very confusing. It was the wrong love and because of that I was happy and sad. My family made me happy. My husband was a "good husband" and provider and our future seemed bright. But nothing had actually changed. We were still the same people. As happy as I was, more often than not, when we were intimate and the lights in the bedroom went off, I would just go through the motions so that it could end quickly. I continued to participate in perverse scenarios for the next few years. I would confide in my good friend Elize from work and she never judged me nor him. I loved that about her. I didn't want her to pick sides.

"When hope's dream seems to drag on and on,
the delay can be depressing."
Proverbs 13:12

As the years went by, I found myself in a good place simply because I had chosen to be happy despite my circumstances. It had become a state of mind; I had many things to be grateful for. I conditioned myself to love my life and accept it at face value. For a while now, my twin had been telling me how blessed she was. She mentioned God from time to time and she was full of happiness that she called joy. She was always upbeat and vibrant; it didn't matter what kind of day it was, to her it was a beautiful day. I wanted that fullness of happiness.

I thought I was happy except when my husband and I were occasionally intimate – when I felt it was not the GOD intended intimacy – I felt disgusted. Strangely, although

I always went along with it, the next day I "forgot" the events of the night before and it was all fine again. This had become our pattern since that first night 13 years before when we were in the Poconos for our first wedding anniversary. It was as if I was under some kind of hypnotic trance similar to what I had experienced during a vacation we took as a family to Mexico, where I would go through something that broke me but a few hours later I would forget and be whole again. I was always ready to please, even if it was at a high cost to me. My whole life I had found solace in writing down my thoughts in journals and letters. I started carrying a small notebook and I tried to make note of the highlight of the day. I figured that no matter what kind of day I had, there must had been at least one good thing that happened. It worked!

Everything was going really well for the past year and I decided to go back to school. The last time I had enrolled in college classes I became pregnant and after a while I could not finish so I was excited to go back to further my education. Things were really looking up, I was optimistic and, as in the past, I was hopeful about my future. I even started working out with a trainer. I was also running again and losing weight. For the first time in my life, I liked the woman staring back in the mirror. I was still seeing my therapist but less frequently now. I continued to reach out and read passages from the Bible that still sat on my night table. I was searching more than ever before. For many years, I had been trying to understand the spirit realm. I would consult my "spirit guide" every now and then and I would read about how the spirit world works and would call on them when I needed "guidance." I was seeking something greater than me but I didn't know what or how to find it so I tried many things. Back then, I hadn't yet realized that which I was seeking was already close to me. Someone had given me a pocket size New Testament Psalm; Proverb Bible and I would try to read it every day even if it was just for a few minutes.

*"For what use is it to gain all the wealth
and power of this world, with everything it
could offer you, at the cost of your own life?"*
Mark 8:36

Tired of being a patrol officer, Hugo decided to take the sergeant's exam. I was so proud of him and did my best to give him his space to study. A couple of times we went together to the library to study. Working a full-time job while attending school was exhausting but I was determined to get ahead! The hard work made me look forward to our next summer vacation even more. We invited my family and it was supposed to be a grand time. We were enjoying our vacation and in between the excursions, you could find us by the pool, drink in hand or by the buffet. One morning, as my sisters and I walked around the resort and saw a wedding gazebo by the beach we talked about how beautiful it must be to get married there. All of a sudden, we started to day dream of what it would be like if Hugo and I renewed our vows at a resort such as this. A wedding and vacation all at once. As we returned to the rest of the group, my twin made an announcement directed at my husband "we just saw where you and my sister are getting married again."

Almost at the end of our vacation, my husband and I had a small argument. Since I had some down time, I thought about many things, especially what happiness meant to me as if something inside me was rebelling. I was feeling good; I had built up my self-esteem. I was confident enough to have a conversation with my husband to finally fix what was wrong with our marriage. I felt I needed to speak up about how degraded I felt during sex. I wanted to pour out my heart and I knew he would understand. I believed he was totally in love with me – he did say I was hot and I'm sure he wouldn't want to jeopardize our relationship. This time, I knew he would make the effort to change. As I ironed my clothes for dinner, I played out different scenarios in my head of how the conversation would go as I told him that I no longer wanted to hear about his fantasies. The fantasies that made me feel dirty and disgusting toward myself and toward him. I knew I was not perfect, and my complacency perhaps allowed it to go on further. Nevertheless, I felt I was being taken advantage of; I was manipulated into doing things I regretted. I had spent my whole life in a search of true love, confused because I had searched in the wrong places. I had been promiscuous as a teenager and also as an adult, I had had multiple extra marital affairs. My past had been used against me in the bedroom; it had become part of my husband's distorted fantasies. I decided to be honest with him. I no longer wanted to talk about my past sexual escapades; nor did I want to make up stories when I no longer had stories to tell.

While at dinner, he made a comment that I did not appreciate, and it confirmed the notion that I had to have that conversation with him. I asked him to take a walk with me on the beach. The walk felt long, and I was very nervous to disclose my heart, but I was hoping for breakthrough in my marriage. Throughout the years, I wrote letters in my journals to God. Some letters were thanking Him for what I had; some were asking for help; others were just me pouring my heart out and letting my pain come to the surface. I felt a strength that was not my own. That night, I knew something would shift and so I intentionally made a mental note of everything. As we sat on the sand, I took notice of how the big moon cast its reflection on the sea, its bright light making it easier for me to fix my eyes on what looked like thousands of fish swimming under the water creating tiny waves on the ocean. It was a beautiful night!

I asked him to please let me speak without interruption and that I would do the same for him. Then, I proceeded to tell him my true feelings. I told him "I am really unhappy at the moment" "I am not happy with the way our marriage is going." I told him how exhausted I was and that I was feeling stressed out with school, work and taking care of the house. That night I wore my heart on my sleeve and left my true emotions on the table. I wasn't venting; I was making him aware of every deep thought. It was clear that I had been playing out this conversation for a while. With tears in my eyes and my voice shaking but with a firm tone, I declared that I no longer wanted to participate in his delusional reality. I took responsibility for my own actions and placed blame where needed. Resolutely, I stated that I would no longer be a participant and I was clearly ready for change.

When I was done talking, I was met with silence. Perhaps he thought I wasn't done, and didn't want to interrupt me, so I asked him if he had anything to say. All he said was "Okay, I understand." I could not believe what I just heard. When I was talking to him just a few minutes earlier, I was hoping that he would put his hand on mine or comfort me but that did not happen. Now at the very least I waited for an apology of some sort or even for him to take some responsibility for his behavior and the state of our marriage. But that did not occur and, after a few minutes of silence, we walked back to meet the rest of the group. During our walk there I asked if we needed time apart and my husband said maybe we did.

The next day while my sisters and the rest of the family went on their final excursion, Hugo and I along with our girls decided to stay at the resort. I was in no mood to go anywhere. We did not talk about the conversation from the night before. We pretended that everything was fine in front of our girls. I was sad but I was okay. I didn't even think much of the last comment he made before we walked back to the group the previous night. It was just another typical day in my life, sweeping everything under the rug. Besides, it was the last full day we would be at the resort. The next day we were heading home and back to the routine, so I enjoyed watching my girls horsing around in the pool. No words can describe the peace that I felt in that moment. That scene was interrupted when everyone else returned from their excursion. They told me how much fun they had and showed me some of the souvenirs they picked up along the way. No one noticed anything was amiss otherwise, they would have commented. We enjoyed our last night of vacation.

Upon returning home, my husband and I hardly spoke. It wasn't like we were arguing; we just did not speak to each other. A couple of days later, on a Friday morning, he left for a motorcycle trip with his work buddies to Ocean City, Maryland for about a week. The next day one of my best friends, Antonio, was having a pool party so my daughters and I spent the day there. Antonio could be a bit conceited and presumptuous but I loved him dearly because he always made me laugh. He had more stories to tell than I did. One of the reasons why we got along so well was because he also had a past and many times we compared stories. While watching the kids splashing in the pool, I told Antonio what transpired during my family vacation. I detailed the conversation with my husband. I told him that since our return, Hugo and I were not speaking other than what was necessary. I mentioned how I hadn't heard from him since the morning before when I wished him a good trip before I left for work. At Antonio's prompting, I called Hugo but he did not answer. That annoyed me. *What if it had been important? What if I needed to talk to him about our girls?* *"Is my marriage over?"* I asked Antonio. He looked at me and said "oh sweetie, stop it." So, we changed the subject and moved on.

When Hugo returned, I was met with the same silence. He did not show any emotion when he saw me. I was disappointed but I did not regret telling him about my feelings. That night when we went to bed, the silence was deafening. I needed to hear his voice talking to me. We needed to talk about whatever was going on between us. I deserved to know. We had a couple of weddings to go to that weekend so I told him that we shouldn't go together to his friend's wedding. I would go to my coworker's wedding and he should go to his friend's. Of course, I did not mean that but I needed to say anything to get a reaction. He told me that he agreed and said:

"You know, Claudia, I don't want to be with you anymore."

It felt like a bucket of ice water slowly being poured over me. I sat up quickly, my heart was racing and confronted him about that statement.

"What are you talking about? Are you telling me that we are done?"

"Yes." he said.

At that, I got out of bed and told him that I needed fresh air and was leaving. I couldn't stay there. I got dressed and as I was about to walk out of the bedroom, I looked at him and asked:

"Are you sure that this is what you want? Because if the answer is yes, I am never coming back."

He nodded and verbally confirmed it at the same time. It was past midnight on July 24, 2009 when I finally had the breakthrough I had been praying for. I made two phone calls: The first one to Antonio to let him know I was on my way to his house because I needed a place for the night. I knew that I didn't have to ask, it was just a formality so that he knew who was ringing the bell so late into the night. The other call was to my co-worker to let her know that I would not be coming in to work the next day.

Antonio and I sat on the couch and crying I told him what had just occurred. My tears were more out of anger than sorrow. I shared with him some of the things I had endured, things that I did that I have to live with. I was mad that I had done so much to please my husband and was manipulated. My marriage was over because I had spoken up? Antonio looked at me and said:

"Sweetie, he is a jerk."

And with that we went to sleep. The next morning, I was up early and it felt like I was in a daze. I called my twin and told her what happened and she was just as upset as I was but somewhat hopeful that we would get back together.

She didn't know all that much about this area of my life. I called Hugo to let him know that we needed to talk and he agreed.

He was cleaning the pool when I got home but since we needed to go to Costco to pick up some stuff, we decided to talk on the ride there. We didn't say much until we parked at the very end of the parking lot. I started the conversation.

"Is there someone else?" "No."

"Is it me?"

"No, Claudia it is not you. Sometimes I feel like getting on my motorcycle and just going for a ride and not coming back." "Are you going through a midlife crisis?"

"No."

"What is it then?"

"I don't know. I just don't want to be married to you anymore." I kept asking questions because I was trying to understand his position. I thought we had been getting better. He told me that he had been unhappy for a while now and didn't want to fake it any more. When I heard those words a sense of peace came over me and I heard a quiet voice in my head telling me that I was going to be okay. I wiped my tears and faced my husband.

"You know what? I release you."

I told him he was free to go. I had spent my life looking for happiness and he deserved to find his happiness as well. I told him I was sorry for missing the signs that he wasn't happy. That last sentiment was sincere and not bitter. I truly was sorry that he wasn't happy. After all, I was feeling the same way. You'd think he'd be happy to hear me say those things but my words must have burned. Rather than thanking me for understanding, voicing relief, or sharing some sentiment, he grew angry.

"What the f^@# was that about? One minute you're crying and the next you're ok? That easy, huh?"

I was taken aback for a second, but I had peace with my decision. We had been unhappy for too long in our broken relationship and we were only getting worse. I reiterated that he deserved to be happy just like I deserved to find happiness and maybe that meant that we left each other. After an awkward silence, we left the car and walked toward the store. When we got into Costco, I headed directly to the bathroom. I was sick to my stomach, literally. I knew in my heart and mind that this time was different. It was truly over.

Chapter Seventeen

NEW BEGINNINGS

*"I will instruct you and teach you in the way
you should go; I will counsel you with my eye upon you."
Psalm 32:8*

That Friday is still a blur. After our Costco run, we went back home and tried to keep up appearances for our girls' sake. Although, I was well used to keeping up false appearances, this time was different. Unbeknownst to me, change was beginning to take place in my heart. To be honest that weekend is still very foggy in my mind. I remember lots of conversations with close friends and family. No matter who was on the other end of the phone, the response to my life–changing news was the same. Every single person was shocked by my words. I wasn't surprised at their reactions. Like I said, I was well used to keeping up false appearances and my husband and I had put up the facade of being a loving couple for years. Trying to comfort, one of my friends told me that we would get back together and I just had to wait. I politely thanked her for her thoughts, but in my heart, I knew there was zero chance of that happening. This time, I was done, and it was time to move on.

It took me two days to move on after the end of 15 years of marriage. Some people mistook my quick recovery as not caring. That couldn't be farther from the truth. I did care. A lot. Only God knows the number of tears I cried but there was no turning back. When I arrived at work the following Monday, I shared the news with one of my co-workers.

"How can you be okay?" She asked.

Her face showed her genuine concern.

"God has given me a brand-new canvas and He is my brush."

My answer shocked me as much as it did her. I had no clue where those words came from, but that became my proclamation. Any time someone asked me how I was doing, I repeated that mantra. They weren't just words. I truly believe that and it simply made me feel stronger on the inside and I saw more of God moving in my life.

Later that evening, I stepped out the backdoor of my house to talk to Hugo. I gave him with a stone-cold look as we talked. I wish I didn't have to see him, but we had to discuss our future plans. He told me he was already looking into moving out, but needed a few weeks before his new apartment would be available. In return, I set up some rules that he would have to follow until he moved out. We wouldn't see each other during the week, we would have to co-exist as housemates on his days off, and we wouldn't discuss anything with the girls until after they returned from visiting their cousins in Florida. In the meantime, we would only talk to discuss the logistics of our divorce. He agreed to these rules and I ended the conversation by walking back in the house. Once inside, I took a breath and released it with a sense of relief. Despite seventeen years of memories, I was happy to let go.

> *"so that we would not be exploited*
> *by the adversary, Satan,*
> *for we know his clever schemes*
> *2 Corinthians 2:11"*

Five days after our conversation, he broke one of my rules. I was already sleeping when he walked through the bedroom door and I woke up when I sensed him laying down next to me, trying to get intimate with me. I was not interested and told him so. He apologized and backed away. The next day, he texted me an apology for "disrespecting" me. I couldn't believe it! Since September 29, 1995, our one-year anniversary, that had been his normal behavior – disrespecting me and my body. Over the next few weeks, he kept trying to get close to me in order to wiggle himself back into my life. He didn't seem to understand that I was over him. The truth was – I was over the dysfunctional and toxic marital relationship we'd had over the last 15 years. I was ready to let go and be truly free...of everything. I had been promiscuous growing up. At 17 years of age, I had gotten involved with a man 17 years my senior. I had been a cheater, an adulterer. I wasn't just done with him; I was done with it all.

This time was a new beginning for me and I felt that he was trying to sabotage it. He was indecisive. He was annoying. It seemed as if his goal was to make this harder for me. He knew what time I would be at the gym and would text me just to say hi. I had enough. At last, I was moving on but I still struggled with the pain and emotion of it all. It was one thing to have hope of a better future, but it was completely another thing to ignore the painful memories as if they had never occurred. It seemed that just as hard as I was trying to move on, he was trying to pull me back. He would call and text me to tell me that he cared for me. He would try to talk sweetly to me when he walked in the house. His words cut deep like a wound. He just didn't get it. The last thing I wanted to hear was the one thing he would never say. I didn't want his sweet words, or his romance. I wanted an apology. An apology for the pain he caused, the shame he made me feel, and the years of subjecting to me to his fantasies. Whether or not he ever said those words to me, I knew I was done. I would no longer lend my body to his sexual satisfactions, his fantasies, his wants and desires. I would no longer lay there during and after he had his way with me – numb to the pain. I told him to only contact me regarding our daughters. As hard as it was, I knew this was for the best.

Remember, I said that he seemed determined to pull me back. I meant that. I remember one day specifically. Nine days after our parking lot talk, it was raining outside, the sound of thunder playing like heaven's drum. I was alone at the house; the girls were still visiting their cousins in Florida. I finally slowed down enough to think about my feelings. I felt lonely. I didn't think about if I loved him anymore, I didn't. But I did miss his companionship, feeling something familiar. And with my girls gone, I really felt alone in our empty house. Three days later, as if he knew I was feeling lonely, he made his move. His intention was to be with me again and he was relentless. No matter how many times I told him to leave me alone, he kept trying to get close to me and I finally had enough.

"I don't care if you don't have a place to stay, you need to leave now!"

My words were full of emotion. I was disgusted. He made me feel little and powerless as he tried to get his way. This was the true him. He never cared about my feelings, just getting what he wanted. This time, however, I stood strong. The next morning, he messaged me again:

"GOD I'M SO MAD AT MYSELF right now i hate being that way im so weak! Im such a **** that i cant even control myself im sorry for txting u but im so mad at me!... I hate knowing i made u feel that way im no better than that **** in Colombia why do i do these things to myself and the people i care about i hate myslf" [sic]

I didn't buy it! I stayed strong. Day by day, things became clearer and I was optimistic. I was becoming stronger not just for my girls (who still were clueless) but also for myself. One day, I went to the movies by myself. This may seem small, but this simple act made me feel powerful and strong. It showed me that I was capable of doing things on my own – something that I had felt I couldn't do before. Yet with the girls gone there was really nothing worth coming home to and I felt defeated; I could do nothing but cry. Standing in my driveway, my eyes would fill up like a pool of salty water and I would feel as if I were drowning. Walking into the house, I would look at pictures of happier times.

These pictures were supposed to make me smile, but they now reminded me of all the bitter times of the past. At this moment, I realized I was living in a bubble.

"You've become a slave in bondage to your sin."
John 8:34

For two weeks I cried every day. Some tears cleansed me, others healed me, I mostly cried because I missed my daughters terribly! It was Friday night, and I was going out dancing. I looked forward to having fun and forgetting about my situation. I decided to spend the night out to avoid him when I returned home. I didn't want him to kill my vibe. Sure enough, when I did get home Saturday morning, he was awake and asked questions he thought he was privy to. Not only did he question what went on the night before, but when I wouldn't answer, he asked me.

"Are you seeing anyone from the gym?"

I remained silent and rolled my eyes. That was the furthest thing from my mind. He became extremely offended.

"You know, Joe and I were talking about you the other night. I was wondering if when you do get married again, if you will invite me to the wedding? Because, I know you always wanted to get married again but I knew I would never give that to you again. Because, you know, I was only in love with you sometimes."

He was very mean! He told me that he felt he made a mistake getting back together five years before. My heart dropped and I became furious. Like a mad woman, I grabbed each picture I took with him and tore it up. Not a single picture escaped. As I ripped them, I told him that I had been stupid to live a lie. Our entire marriage had been a farce! We had fooled people into thinking we were in a typical marriage. His words pierced and penetrated as though he was using a sharp knife. As he saw my response, he stopped dead in his tracks; he cried and apologized. But it was too little, too late! As I tore the last photo, just like that, I felt completely over him. That last drop of poison killed all emotions: good, bad, resentment, anger, hatred, love that I had for him. Suddenly, I felt absolutely nothing for this man.

A few hours later, I was on my way to see my twin in Stanford, Connectitcut. This was a weekend that I had been looking forward to all week. Even across the miles, she had been there for me. We talked every day, even several times a day. We had made plans to meet her coworkers and go bar hopping. I was mostly excited to see my sister, niece and nephew. Especially after what had happened earlier that day, I definitely needed company. I spoke to my girls and they were playing in the pool with their cousins and were having a great time. They did not suspect anything at all.

When I arrived at my sister's place, she was getting ready. I proceeded to tell her what happened early in the day. She was irate.

"How dare he!?"

However, in the midst of the pain, I was glad that it had happened because it was exactly what I needed. With that, she started to tell me about the date she went on the night before. My sister was beaming with happiness. I loved to see her this happy. My sister's life had been very hard, but she persevered and did what was necessary to provide for my niece and nephew. She had her share of bad breakups, but she was living her best life. I used to love hearing about her dates because I always admired her resilience. She told me about the change in plans. She was going to see her guy friend again that night. We were not going out with her coworkers. I told her I would pass – I didn't want to be the third wheel. I was fine. My sister pleaded with me to come out and I finally conceded.

"You are not setting me up on a blind date, right?"

She promised that she would never do that, so I complied and joined them.

When her date came to pick us up, I could see why my twin sister had been smitten. He was funny, confident, and good looking but more than anything, I could see that he was also smitten by her. When we arrived at the bar, I sat next to my sister and she sat across from her date. They tried to include me in their conversation and not make me feel left out but clearly, they were on a date and I was in the way. I did not want to be there as much as they perhaps wished I wasn't there. Her date got up a few times from the table and finally when I questioned him, he told me that he had been on the phone. He was very nice, and I actually felt bad to have been rude to him when he tried to find something in common with me. He had rolled up his sleeve and showed me a tattoo that he was so proud of. I made a joke about it, but I came off as presumptuous. Once more he excused himself and told my sister he had to make another call. When he returned, he announced that one of his friends, Dave, was coming out to meet us. *Great!* I thought. Before midnight, as we were enjoying the hot summer night outside the bar, my sister's date gestured his friend to come over. I saw him approaching us and without thinking I said:

"What the hell took you so long?"

Unfazed by my rudeness, Dave answered with a smile.

"I was at the Yankees game."

And with that I made a joke and we all laughed. This friend was tall and had beautiful tanned skin. My initial thought was that he was nice and I was relieved that he could keep me company while my sister enjoyed her date.

"For if you embrace the truth,
it will release more freedom into your lives."
John 8:23

Finally, someone to talk to and have a great time. The night was still young, and I wanted to enjoy it as much as I could. Dave and I started with formalities and small talk. The more he spoke, the more I wanted him to continue. Here was this gentle giant laughing at my stupid jokes and sarcasm. It was amazing! We decided to take it to the dance floor, I wrapped my arms around his neck as he placed his big hands around my waist as we danced. We danced for a while before we decided to leave together. We spent the night together but not as you may think...The intent was there, but we talked more than anything. I was completely honest with this man I just met. I do not know what prompted that. Perhaps I wanted to scare him off. If he knew what you already do, wouldn't you run? But he didn't. The most beautiful part of that night was the respect; Dave did not try to take advantage of me. I was vulnerable but it felt good to tell my story to this stranger and he also shared his. Several hours later, we walked to the diner for breakfast and we continued talking about life. When we were about to leave, he asked if he could see me again and I said no. I told him it had been one good night. Did he forget what I had shared earlier? He was kind, but persistent.

"Give me one chance. Let me take you on a proper date and if afterwards you never want to see me again, I will respect that."

I accepted.

One date turned into another date and then another. Shortly after, I pressured my soon to be ex-husband to move out, but his apartment would not be available for a couple of months. I was frustrated and annoyed. I did not want to see him unless it was absolutely necessary. He noticed my change in behavior and noticed a new sparkle in my eye. He was unbearable to be around with his crude jokes and stupid comments.

When my daughters came back from their visit with family, we sat down with them to tell them about our decision to divorce. As you can imagine that was not an easy conversation. I had spent my entire time as a mom trying to do all I could to protect them from pain. Now, I was part of inflicting heartache and grief on them. After all, I fully understood what it was like to not have your parents together. I was hurting for them and with them. However, throughout this season, I continued to pray and thank God for answering my prayers and for giving me strength. My daughters meant everything to me but there was nothing I could do. There was no other way.

On what would have been our fifteenth wedding anniversary, I sat down and wrote in my journal about the many memories that we shared as a married couple. Not all memories were bad. In fact, the good memories outweighed the not so good. It was for those memories that I cried. In my journal I also wrote, despite the tears that were falling, I was no longer feeling hurt anymore. I had been released from those shackles. At last, I had enough courage to take a stand and keep the promise that I made the night he said it was over. For the first time ever in my entire existence, a man made me feel loved and cared for. This new man in my life, Dave, who came in at the worst time was the most compassionate man I had ever known. The more I got to know him, the more grateful I was.

Chapter Eighteen

TRUE LOVE

*"For I know the plans I have for you,
declares the Lord, plans for welfare and not for evil,
to give you a future and a hope"
Jeremiah 29:11*

Eventually, Hugo moved out and we made arrangements concerning the girls. These two girls were my strength. The last thing I ever wanted to do was hurt them; I was scared that they would grow up and be deeply affected by the divorce. I did not want my treasures to have trust issues as adults but this was the best thing I could do for them. With him out of the house, I had to figure out another source of income. Although he was providing child support, it would not be enough. I eventually rented my finished basement to a single mom and her toddler daughter. For a while, before Hugo and I had decided to separate, I had a part time job selling sensual items but that was the old me and I had stopped.

Not long after I met Dave, he said he was in love with me. It seemed insane because we had been dating for only a few weeks. But that is exactly how it happened – in a few short weeks, we were in love. This was the first time those words were said with pure meaning. Whenever Dave looked at me, he did so in amazement as if I was some kind of strange creature. In his eyes I am the most beautiful woman on earth. It was impossible not to reciprocate those feelings. We found ways to see each other every day. We met often at my local bakery for coffee and a pastry. Other days we met at the local restaurant for drinks. We would go on picnics to the beach and talk about our children and make plans for them to meet one day soon. We talked about whether they would get along. We liked to dream.

I wanted to do something nice for my girls since they were going through so much. I took them to Salem, Massachusetts during the Halloween weekend. We couldn't contain our excitement the minute we got in the car. We played music and we talked. Their state of heart was so important – I needed to make sure that they were okay. As they answered certain questions, it seemed they were well with the new arrangements. That night after check-in, we went to the pool.

As I watched my daughters play in the water, I realized this was the first weekend trip with just the three of us. It was a fun weekend that was almost ruined as I blurted out some news about the new man in my life. You can imagine their reaction and rightfully so. I had been carrying so many secrets for so many years; even hidden much from them that perhaps without thinking I wanted to just be forthcoming. We wiped our tears, hugged, kissed and leaned on each other for the rest of the weekend. To this day, we laugh about it – my girls have joked that I took them away that weekend to break the news about my boyfriend and no one will change their minds.

Shortly after, when Dave and I were on our way to his house to pick something up, we passed his mother and oldest daughter in the car. I remember how this young beautiful girl smiled at him and waved at us. I had a grin from ear to ear; I could not wait to meet her. A few days later, I met his youngest daughter. She saw my high heels and told me they were pretty.

They were bright red with white polka dots; they reminded her of her favorite character, Minnie Mouse. When I met Dave's son, he gave me a genuine smile while waving hello.

One night, this not so new man came to pick me up and, out of nowhere, Ariel said that he should come inside because she wanted to meet him. I was shocked and elated at the same time. She wanted to meet the guy I was excited about. Dave was pleasantly surprised when I asked him to come in. They were both nervous when they came face to face. Dave stuttered a little while introducing himself. As Ariel began to speak, she was about to sit on the arm of the couch and totally missed it and fell down. My poor girl. We all started laughing. That's how Ariel broke the ice, with her fall! Eventually, Samantha and Ariel asked more questions about him and his kids and so did Dave's children. We asked them if they wanted to meet and they agreed. We met at Dave & Busters and slowly made conversations over dinner. There were a couple of uncomfortable moments but that was to be expected. We had a great time that day because the kids got along. I thanked God for putting "a wonderful, caring, handsome and incredible man" in my life and I loved spending time with all of them together.

During winter break, my soon to be ex-husband took our girls to Florida, and I was a mess. I cried almost every day because I missed them so much. That Christmas Eve, Dave invited me to spend it with his family. I was conflicted. I wanted to stay home and cry – I missed my girls so much and this was the first Christmas we wouldn't be spending together. I was happy for them; they were having a blast with their cousins in Florida but as for myself, I was miserable without them. Our first holiday together afforded me the opportunity to see another side of the new man in my life. This gentle giant had gone through hundreds of pictures of his family and carefully selected the most genuine ones to frame as gifts. I did join Dave and his family for Christmas Eve and though I was made to feel welcomed by everyone, I was very sad inside. At one point during the evening, I excused myself to go to the bathroom and sat on the cold floor and cried. I longed to be with my girls so much. After a while I freshened up and retouched my make-up then rejoined everyone else. No one knew the sorrow I felt that night except Dave and he did all he could to make me feel better. As the new year rolled in, we were making plans for 2010 and what it would bring; our plans included each other. It was crazy that after just four months of meeting each other we were talking about the details of a possible future together.

The next day my twin and I were eager to hear about each other's evenings. Life was very good – I found myself in God's presence more often and my twin sister helped me recognize that. That year Dave and I started creating many memories with our children together, many times including my niece and nephew. We became one big happy family in-training. I was totally enamored with him. This man took my feelings into consideration. Whenever Dave noticed that I was hurting, he was there.

I took my girls to Puerto Rico the following summer to celebrate Samantha's sixteenth birthday and Dave met us there. This was our first vacation together and it was perfect. Their bond was getting tighter and I could tell they genuinely cared for each other.

When the girls' dad took them on a cruise vacation, I became melancholy. I missed them and I was inconsolable. My schoolwork also contributed to my stress and missing my girls made it worse. One day while Dave was visiting, he called me over to the room and handed me the phone. Samantha was on the phone saying hi. I was speechless that this considerate man went out of his way to reach my daughters by phone in the middle of their cruise so I could hear their voices. What did I do to deserve such a kind man?

Meanwhile, I was struggling to make ends meet and though I felt super comfortable with Dave, I never let on with my financial challenges. Hugo was providing child support, but I was going through hardship. Perhaps it was pride, but I even sold every piece of jewelry that I owned and did not ask anyone for help. I was sad and sometimes I cried when I sold a few of my pieces that had sentimental value but that quickly subsided, and I moved on. Except Christmas of that year. When he was almost done with his shopping, Dave asked me if there was anything I was getting for my girls and I told him "not now." I played it off as if I hadn't found anything interesting at the store. Truth be told – I had no money and I was brokenhearted. Had I been honest with him, no doubt Dave would have done all the shopping for me, but I did not dare. I struggled a lot at first because I wanted this relationship to work but I didn't think I was worthy of such happiness. Many times, I foolishly tried to sabotage our relationship, but Dave never gave up on us.

In 2011, two years after we met, we talked about moving in together. Samantha and Ariel did not oppose. They had grown very fond of each other. Dave and my daughters had each other's backs. When I got annoyed at him, they came to his rescue and when I got annoyed at the girls, he rescued them. I could never win but I wouldn't have it any other way. Before the beginning of the school year in 2011, Dave moved in with us. My ex and I were meeting with a mediator and our divorce was civil. Everything was very amicable between us and I learned to ignore his occasional sexual advances. He was very remorseful and decided to give up the house, but should I sell it one day, I would split it with each of our girls. December 2011, the judge signed our divorce papers.

Dave grew up in the Catholic faith so we went to church on all the special holidays but when we moved in together, we decided to start attending church more often. I wept every time the priest mentioned the name of Jesus. I don't know why but I always wept. It wasn't intentional but without fail, I would be overtaken by emotions and without warning, tears would form. As I reflect back it is yet another sign of the lengths to which He was pursuing me.

March 8, 2012, Dave and I were going away for a long weekend. Our flight to Florida was delayed but it didn't matter to us because nothing was going to ruin the next few days. By the time we got to the condo, I was exhausted and ready for bed. However, Dave insisted that we go for a walk on the beach. While we walked, we talked about the future and before I knew it, he was on one knee asking me to be his wife. I said "YES!"

Chapter Nineteen

WHIRLWINDS

"Forget the former things; do not dwell on the past.
See, I am doing a new thing!
Now it springs up; do you not perceive it?"
Isaiah 43:18-19

W e were both beyond excited to be engaged. Everyone was thrilled for us when they heard the news about our engagement. Friends and family were no longer skeptical about our new relationship. Now, those closest to me could understand why I had fallen so quick and so hard for this man. There were many qualities that contributed to such rushed feelings. Dave respected me and my needs were his priority. We talked about our previous marriages and mistakes, but more importantly, we talked about how we would not repeat those mistakes in the future. I believed him. When we had first started dating, out of what I can only describe as emotional muscle memory, I tried to push the boundaries and bring some of my past into our relationship. He kindly and gently reminded me that he was different. Dave was not interested nor willing to accept misbehaviors from me. Not that I wanted to! I finally knew real happiness and I traded my tears of sadness for joy. I could not believe the happiness that I was being offered.

"The sun rises and the sun sets;
And hurrying to its place it rises there again"
Ecclesiastes 1:5

The months that followed our engagement were a whirlwind of excitement. We began to plan our wedding and as if that wasn't enough, my family started having issues and coming to us for help. It started with my younger brother, who is a product of my mom's third marriage and is 19 years younger than me. He kept getting in trouble at school in Georgia. I asked Dave if my brother could move in with us. Without hesitation, he welcomed my youngest brother to stay with us. Since my brother was just a few years older than my daughters, they enjoyed getting to spend time with their older "cousin." They didn't care to explain that he was their uncle. Shortly after my brother moved in, I got a call from my oldest sister in Georgia. By her tone of voice, I knew it was serious.

"Claudia, mom had two biopsies and they both matched. She has been diagnosed with lymphoma."

Hearing these words, I sat at my desk and cried. Poor mom! She had taken the news of my divorce hard. Now, finally, after getting over that, she received this news. I spoke with my fiancé, my siblings and my mom; we decided that it would be best for her to come and live with us. Our fully finished basement was now tenant free, which was perfect for my mom to move into our two-bedroom basement. That weekend, I caught a flight to Georgia to pick up my mom. After getting her situated, I immediately started calling around to make her appointments. The surgeons at the hospital where I worked had a great reputation and I knew them well. Even though the circumstances were not the best, I was glad my mom had come to stay with us. I didn't view any of this happening as an accident. God was bringing us all together for a reason. Maybe He knew it was time for my family to come back together or maybe He wanted to do something with us. I wasn't sure, but I knew it was a good thing. Anyway, with the family all together, we attacked planning our wedding and my mom's healthcare all at the same time. After weeks of deliberating, we decided to have a destination wedding at a resort in Punta Cana in the Dominican Republic. I would have my beach wedding after all!

A few days after mom's move, we met with an oncologist for a second opinion. The doctor confirmed her diagnosis; it was in a aggressive stage. The MRI showed a tumor on her pelvis that needed a biopsy, but he couldn't do it. After that appointment, I took my mom to my office and we spoke to another surgeon. He reviewed the images and agreed with the oncologist. When I asked if he could do the surgery to remove the tumor mom had in her pelvis, the surgeon explained that this was beyond his capability, but he called one of his colleagues who specialized in complicated cases and she agreed to see us right away. I knew this surgeon well and I was relieved to know that she would be able to help my mom.

After a brief consult and review of the images, the doctor said it was impossible to get the tumor out from my mom's pelvis. In fact, the surgeon explained that in order for her to get to the tumor, she would have to "remove her pelvis, put it on the table and take out the tumor. Impossible." Needless to say, I was devastated. My mom, on the other hand, was calm throughout the entire day. I am sure she was worried, but she remained calm. She said she had faith that she would be healed. I didn't understand her but I admired her optimism. I was not as optimistic. To the contrary, I was sad and I felt so guilty for the things I had put her through. I had not been an easy teenager nor good daughter. With a simple prayer, I asked God to heal her even though I didn't really believe in such things, not quite yet. After the disappointing meetings indicating there were no options, I took her to Memorial Sloan Kettering Cancer Center. She was seen and for now, the main focus was the lymphoma since there was nothing really to do about the tumor. Her new doctor wanted to review the slides from the biopsies before making recommendations. In the meantime, I could see my mom losing weight and she was fatigued and out of breath all the time. I could actually feel her lymph nodes under her skin. I was scared.

By this time, my twin had been living about five minutes away from me. She had also found her knight in shining armor and now, they had a son together. Both my mom and my twin went to church together on Sunday and they constantly asked me to tag along. Running out of excuses not to go, I finally accepted their invitation and went with them to a Christian church. It was a different experience. I felt something beautiful inside of me. The music was lively and the message relevant to life. I looked around and the people were moved by the worship and most of them had their hands raised and tears on their faces. Peace was something I had searched for so long in my life; I lived with so much regret. Inside I struggled with my past. All of it. The guilt had always plagued me and standing there I asked for forgiveness. Before the service came to an end, the pastor invited those who wanted to pray for salvation. Broken from past pain, I walked forward with many others and repeated the words the pastor recited as I continued to cry. When I returned to my seat, my mom and sister were crying as well. I wish I could tell you that after that Sunday I noticed a change in how I felt but I didn't. I still had regret and remorse for my actions and so the next time I went to church, I walked to the front and repeated the prayer of salvation once again.

A few days before my mom's appointment to go over treatment options, I was upstairs sweeping the floor when my mom came rushing up the basement stairs. She was pale and sweating. I was alarmed and asked: "what's wrong?" She could hardly get the words out but finally told me that she had been praying with my brother.

"We felt the Holy Spirit come down and like a rushing wind. He left. I know I have been healed from cancer."

I was incredulous and sad because I didn't want my mom's hopes to be high only to be disappointed when we met with the doctor the following week. While my mom was still talking, my brother came up the stairs as well and could hardly wait to tell me what he had just witnessed. He repeated what my mom had just described. I nodded in total disbelief. That afternoon, my sister stopped in for a visit. As we talked about our mom's health, my sister said she wasn't all that worried because my mom was already healed. WHAT?!! I practically yelled at her for the nonchalant tone when she spoke those words. I was the one taking mom to all of her appointments. Clearly, she did not understand the severity of her condition. Two biopsies had confirmed mom's cancer but now everyone in my family decided they knew better than the doctors.

I was irate to say the least and I let her know it. How could they be so naïve?

"And the prayer of faith will save the one who is sick, and the Lord will raise him up...."

James 5:15

On January 15, 2013, my mom and I went to the cancer center to hear the possible options for her treatment. I was a ball of nerves! When the doctor came into her office, she took her hand from her coat pocket and shook mine. After a few formalities, I asked her to lay it down for us. I was fully prepared to hear the worst news. I honestly cannot describe the doctor's demeanor. She began to tell us that she had no explanation for what she was about to say:

"Your mother's lymphoma has turned into granuloma."

She continued to explain that from the looks of the biopsy, mom's lymph nodes were now filled with fat. In other words, she was cured.

"I know, God healed me." My mom said after hearing the doctor's words.

I don't' know if the doctor believed in God, but she still nodded her head in silent agreement. There really was no other explanation to this miracle.

"I told you!" my twin exclaimed when we shared the news with her that evening. I was so thankful to God yet

I was quite skeptical. I kept thinking how the doctors had been wrong. Maybe they had made a mistake with the initial biopsies? That was the only logical explanation. Right? While my family was excited and sure of what they saw, I still wasn't convinced.

Following this event, I renewed by my search for something more in life. I had seen too many people, including my family, that seemed to live a life filled with happiness and hope despite their circumstances. It was time I found that for myself. I was still in bondage and struggling with some demons. Again, I told my sister that I would join them at church on the following Sunday. I was being tormented with shame and guilt; yet I was still feeling drawn to the God she knew, and I needed to be in "His presence"–that lured me to go with her to church. That Sunday, the pastor of this new church took a good look at me and while he was preaching, he managed to bring up the topic of tattoos in his message and flat out looked at me and said that tattoos are a sin against God. I felt extremely judged and was taken aback; I wanted to run away from there but I couldn't. *Was this true? How could such a thing be?* I was confused. Again, when they made the call for salvation, I went forward and wept while they prayed over me. I mean if tattoos are a sin, I wanted forgiveness! Again, for the third time, I repeated the prayer for salvation, still nothing changed.

A few months later, Dave mentioned that his job was offering a great career opportunity in Japan. This was the second time he had been asked to go and they expected him to make his decision soon. It wasn't much of a choice really and this project was to last for six months. It was a relocation with all expenses paid and I would accompany him. I was ecstatic. We spent the next few days talking about it and figuring out the details. We would have to leave my girls with my ex-husband. *Would he agree?* We hoped Hugo would temporarily move in and look after the girls. I knew this would be a huge ask but we were on really good terms and were getting along, plus he would jump at any opportunity to spend more time with them. As expected, after explaining our predicament, my ex-husband agreed to stay at the house to look after our girls while Dave and I traveled overseas after our wedding. Despite our differences, we both shared a love for the girls and would do anything to take care of them. Everything was in place; everything was working out. My fiancé's job made it possible for me to travel along and even paid for my visa and travel expenses. Samantha and Ariel had mixed emotions, but understood why we were leaving. We knew it wouldn't be easy; we had never been apart this long. The longest had been for a month or so while they visited family in Florida. If that had been hard, imagine being apart for six months, on different sides of the world and with a 13-hour time difference. There would be so much to get used to.

Dave and I were extremely grateful for Hugo's help. In spite of so much, my relationship with Hugo had been amicable once we decided to file for divorce. Since the day that decision was made, we vowed to get along and make our daughters our priority. I never once portrayed their dad in a negative light; there wasn't anything negative to say about him to them. He had always been a great father. His love and devotion for our girls was evident and this needed to continue despite our separation. Even with our commitment to make it work – it was still difficult for them. My oldest daughter took it quite hard. So much so, that at one point during the first year I saw how she struggled with her emotions and I questioned whether or not we had made the right decision. It was during those moments that I wished I could take her pain away and even regretted speaking up. I grew up with the repercussions of years of abuse and the feeling of being unworthy of true love. I felt the guilt of this broken marriage and my goal was to ensure that my girls would not see their parents in a bitter divorce. There was no need. Besides, time had revealed many things to their dad and he was finally sorry for his wrongdoings in our marriage and I was as well. Since our split, we've become better people. We both reflected a lot on our actions and took responsibility for all we had done.

One Tuesday afternoon, in the middle of this whirlwind of events, Dave called me and asked if we had plans for Saturday?

"No. Why?" I asked.

"Do you want to get married this weekend?"

It didn't take much convincing. I said yes. I had been planning our wedding in Punta Cana, DR for months. The invitations had been sent out and most of the RSVPs received. I had been counting the days to say I do. Our wedding was about a month away, but since we were getting married outside the country, a lot of friends wouldn't be able to make it. We went through our guest list and called our friends who would not be able to join us the following month in the Dominican Republic. Everyone said yes and no one was surprised that it was a spur of moment decision. At the time, Dave was a disciple of a Shaolin Monk and so we were honored to be legally married by Shifu Shi Yan Ming on June 9, 2013! It was a beautiful backyard wedding with lace overlay on round tables adorned with candles and wildflowers. I may not have had too much time to plan but as soon as I got off the phone that Tuesday, I went on a shopping spree. At the wedding my twin and her date from the night Dave and I met gave a toast and recounted that fateful night's events. It was meant to be they said. My husband and I agreed. We were meant to be.

Since we were already married, our July wedding in the Caribbean would be symbolic – a moment to share with our families and close friends. Every single detail was perfect from the bright summer colors for the bridesmaids' dresses and bouquets down to the candy bar that read: "Isn't love sweet." It was such a wonderful moment. Picture spending a weeklong vacation with 50 of your loved ones. It was a riot! Every night you could find us at the club, bar, or resort lobby laughing and giggling over silly things, just enjoying life. Just as special as celebrating our marriage, we were also celebrating my mom. She was healed and this was also the first real vacation she had ever taken in her entire life!

On July 12, 2013, my daughters walked me down the aisle for the second time and with the blue ocean as our backdrop, Dave and I promised each other to be faithful, to be each other's supporter and encourager, to always be each other's best friend. I ended my vows calling him "my spiritual partner and the man God meant for me." After the ceremony, first dance, toast and dinner, we were ready to party! It was well past 10:00 pm when the photographer asked if we planned to cut the cake and if we wanted him to capture it in pictures. We had been on the dance floor the entire night and totally forgot about the cake. Of course, we needed pictures cutting the cake and as the photographer started to snap away, a cake fight broke out! We all wore the cake on our faces and clothes and we could not have laughed any harder. Later, we discovered the culprit who started it all—my youngest stepdaughter. Hilarious! Our second wedding was not what I had expected because I could not have pictured such happiness if I tried. By the end of the night, as we rode the trollies back to our rooms, we were exhausted. If there was any doubt of the amazing time we had, just one look at our smiles and the hardening cake on our faces and hair would confirm it.

Chapter Twenty

FINDING GOD IN JAPAN

*"I pray that the eyes of your heart may
be enlightened in order that you may know
the hope to which he has called you, the riches
of his glorious inheritance in his holy people."*
Ephesians 1:18

The following morning, we traveled to another resort to start our honeymoon. My new in-laws had kindly paid for us to spend a week-long honeymoon at an exclusive resort also in Punta Cana. Coming back from our honeymoon, we stayed at my in-laws' home. By now, Hugo had already moved into my house to look after our girls as my husband and I prepared to travel overseas. We spent the next few weeks preparing for our trip. I said goodbye to my co-workers and thanked my supervisor for the opportunity she had given me. My nine years at the hospital had been an amazing time of personal growth. Starting from the bottom, I had developed my skills and worked my way to division supervisor. However, that chapter of my life was closing; they would not be able to hold my position until I came back from my six-month excursion.

On August 14, 2013, we embarked on a new journey. I thought that this trip was all about my husband and his job. I expected to just tag along for the experience. What I would find out as our trip continued was that this was a time for building. Building my relationship with my husband and with God.

Since my husband and I got together, we had become an instant family. Surrounded by our beautiful children, we never had the opportunity to be alone. Although I was excited to travel the world, I was heavy hearted to leave my beautiful family behind. I consoled myself with plans to talk daily, convinced that the time would pass quickly. Still, it was hard to say goodbye.

After our 14-hour trip, we arrived at Narita Airport. We were ready to make this country our home for the next few months. Exiting the airport, I was already fascinated with my surroundings. Everything looked different. The people, the different language on the signs, and most noticeably, the cleanliness. Everything seemed so clean. I couldn't wait to go out and explore! When we arrived at the hotel room, I was shocked at how tiny it was! My 6'1" husband went to the bathroom and could only see half his face in the mirror. We busted out laughing. We went to bed and woke up the next day severely jet-lagged, but that would not keep us from exploring our new home. I was like a kid at an amusement park – I wanted to experience everything. This was a once- in-a-lifetime opportunity and I wanted to take full advantage of it. My husband and I have always been foodies and Japanese cuisine is one of our favorites. We were determined to try everything the country had to offer.

One afternoon, after walking the streets of Tokyo, we stopped at a Chinese Restaurant in Shibuya for lunch. We had already learned by trial and error that the best thing to do was to order food based on the pictures in the menu. The place smelled so delicious; it made our stomachs rumble with hunger. When the server came to take our order, we pointed to the beef and broccoli picture as well as rice and a few other items. While we waited patiently for the food, my husband and I talked about how lucky we were to be there. We talked about how much our children would love it there as well. However, we were glad that it was just the two of us since we were still in our honeymoon season.

When the food arrived, it looked incredible and the smell was amazing, we couldn't wait to dig in. My husband was the first to take a big bite of the beef with broccoli and as fast as it went into his mouth, he spat it out. It was not beef at all but liver! He hates liver. I am not a fan but I ate it growing up in Colombia and figured when in Rome…I ate most of it until I couldn't anymore. We laughed so hard on our way home and vowed to order food when we knew for certain what we were ordering.

The following Monday my husband reported to work to start his new assignment, which meant that I was on my own. Lucky for me, the hotel was next to his office and he would stop by every so often to check up on me. I have to admit that I was a bit too intimidated to wander off on my own; so, for the most part I stayed in that tiny hotel room until he was home. About 2 weeks later, we were told the apartment we would call home for the next few months would be ready. One evening after Dave finished work, we ventured out to our new neighborhood, Shinagawa. As soon as we got off the train and into the station, I was in love. I was amazed by it all and we hadn't even walked outside! Eventually, we made our way toward our new place, stopping first at a Spanish restaurant for dinner. We ordered our food and when it arrived, we looked under our plates to see where the rest of the food was, we would have to adjust to Japanese portions. It was hilarious. We had ordered tapas style but it was like tapas for one: one rib…ONE rib! The menus said ribs, plural. We learned to hang on tightly to each moment that made us laugh.

When we moved out of the hotel into our new apartment, I was impressed. It was smaller than I was accustomed to, but the amenities were very nice. On the top floor of the building was a spa and gym. I was super excited about the gym. In the whirlwind of meeting my husband, I traded my gym time for coffee shops and lattes. The building was also filled with other expats who had left their countries to live in Japan, so we fit right in. I was eager to use this time to reinvent myself. I had always worked for a living and had become a mom and wife at a young age so I looked forward to the next few months of solitude to figure out my passion. I was ready to put myself first. This meant taking care of myself physically. I was ready to get back to the gym. That excitement was short-lived when I was informed that because I have tattoos, I was not allowed to go to the spa or the gym unless I covered them up! Either way, I was happy to make our tiny studio as homey as possible. I displayed pictures of our family and other things that reminded us of home.

About a month later, I started feeling extremely lonely. I missed my daughters; I missed home so much. Samantha was also struggling with feelings of loneliness at school, and it was difficult to comfort her because I felt the same way. I refused to confide in her because I didn't want to add to her stress. Not much longer after that, I began to feel that the trip was a mistake. I knew that I would miss being away from home but didn't anticipate how much. It seemed silly but I missed the little things like the couch and the kitchen counter. I felt so foolish thinking about such things. I found myself crying all the time while Dave was at work. I was so homesick! I started feeling more depressed and the thought of being there for another four months made it worse. I believed I was becoming a burden to my husband.

Dave noticed my changed behavior and encouraged me to go out, which I did but just for short walks. He tried hard to help me cope but nothing worked. We had even enrolled in classes to learn the basics of Japanese so I could go out with more confidence. I was still dealing with the demons inside of me, so many skeletons in my closet, the shame was unbearable. Though I was still taking my antidepressants, they weren't as effective as before and I was fully aware of it.

Eventually, at my husband's urging, I decided to look for a job to keep me busy. I sent my resume to an agency and the next day I received an email inviting me to come in for a meet and greet. The day after that meeting, I received another email to interview at an international school as a teaching assistant. The interview was set for the following week. I wish I could say that I was excited to go, but I wasn't.

I had made it very clear to my husband that I would go to please him not because I was looking forward to it.

"In him we were also chosen,
having been predestined according to the
plan of him who works out everything in conformity
with the purpose of his will"
Ephesians 1:11

On October 11, 2013, I made sure to wear long sleeves to cover my sunflower tattoo for my interview at LoV Preschool. I did not want to blow my chances of getting the job; I knew my husband was right and I needed a distraction. The school principal had given me detailed instructions on how to find the school but I knew it would be challenging still because all the signs would be in Japanese. I downloaded the train app so at least I knew how to get to the train station where I needed to get off. I figured that once I got there, I would just follow Google maps and walk until I made it to my destination. I was ready. After my Japanese class, I made my way to the train station, phone in hand and headphones on. I had just enough time to make it to my interview. I walked up the platform while I waited for the train the app indicated. No sooner had I made it up to the platform than a Middle Eastern man started to make his way toward me. Since arriving two months prior, no one had approached me and this made me feel uncomfortable. He said something but I didn't want to be bothered so I ignored him at first. I thought to myself: *out of all the people here, why does he have to talk to me?* He was persistent and kept on until I took my headphones out to listen to him. He asked me in perfect English: "Do you know how to get to Toda-Koen?" *Oh,* I thought, *he needs help. He also doesn't speak Japanese.* "Yes" I said. "That is where I am going" It was such a coincidence because it was over an hour away from the city! He and I were heading in the same direction. I showed him the app, which explained the train we needed to take. He looked at me and said: "That is not how you get there." *What?* I was confused and annoyed at the same time. If he knew where to go and how to get there, then why was he asking me? He walked over to a train conductor who was in the middle track waiting for passengers to board his train and started speaking in Japanese! He then turned to me and said: "Follow me, I can help you get there. I am getting off two stops before your stop." I was so baffled because this did not make any sense to me. This stranger had specifically asked me if I knew "how to get to Toda-Koen" to then tell me that his stop was two stops before? I did not know what to think but I didn't want to be late for my interview and despite having some reservations, something told me to follow him. We boarded the upcoming train and when he got off to switch train lines, he motioned for me to get off and follow and I did. Then when I saw him get off for the second time, he nodded and reminded me to stay for two more stops, so I did. All the while, still pondering how any of this made any sense. After getting off at the Toda- Koen station in Saitama, I followed Google maps and made my way to the school.

As soon as I walked in, I was overtaken with emotions at the sight of so many children! Immediately after, I noticed all the signs throughout the school. They were bible verses: "Your word is a lamp to guide my feet and a light for my path" Psalms 119:105. There was another sign that read, "He has made everything beautiful in its time" Ecclesiastes 3:11. One that said: "God is Love." I realized that this was a Christian School.

I met with the Principal and Vice Principal of the school, an African couple who had gone to "Japan to bring the Good News to the little children." What a beautiful encounter that was. These two strangers were kind to me; there was something extremely calming about them. It felt relaxed, kind of like listening to a stream from a river flowing freely while hitting rocks. I found them inspirational and motivational. There was something beautiful about them, an essence that I didn't possess.

The interview was going great. I explained to Mrs. Pauline that though I had no experience and English was my second language I had an excellent work ethic. I told her how much I love children. In fact, I told her that I knew I was the right candidate for the job because being a mom has been the greatest reward in life. Looking around the room and seeing all the children's faces, tears started to fall down my own. I was overwhelmed with emotions and I could not contain myself. At that moment, I wanted to be there, not just that day but I felt a sense of urgency to work there. The school was far from home, you could see Mt. Fuji in the distance on my way there, but I thought the commute would give me the opportunity to catch up on some reading. They went over the responsibilities of the role, the pay and hours. They asked about my faith and I explained that I knew of God, that I believed in Him but we didn't have a relationship. The question didn't bother me because I was interviewing at a Christian school. Just before we were wrapping it up, my sleeve went up a bit and exposed my tattoo. Mrs. Pauline's eyes widened and she turned to her husband then back to me and told me:

"If you work here, you have to cover your tattoo."

I explained to her that would not be a problem. She mentioned that the school would provide a shirt, but I needed to wear a long sleeve underneath. I knew I blew it but there was nothing I could do other than reassure them that they would not regret giving me a chance. I also informed them that I was only staying in the country for a few months. I needed to be as honest as possible so they could make an informed decision. I was told they had more candidates coming to interview and they would select the most qualified candidate that same week and get back to me regardless.

On my way home, I replayed the events of that day. I kept thinking of the man I met hours earlier who was heaven sent. Without this encounter, I would have missed the interview. I was cautious not to get too excited, but I was, nonetheless. I couldn't wait to tell my husband!

I was on the bus when my phone rang and it was Mr. Robert. He told me that I had made quite the impression and they wanted to offer me the job. However, I needed to get my working papers. As a resident on a spousal visa, I was allowed to work a certain number of hours a week and I needed to bring that paper with me the following week otherwise they would have to move onto the next candidate.

"Of course," I said. "Anything else?

"No, we are looking forward to have you onboard."

Wahoo! I was so thankful to God for that total stranger who came up to me and convinced me to follow him instead of the app. Still, it didn't make sense how he asked me for directions to ultimately be the one who showed me where I needed to go! My husband took me out to dinner to celebrate my new job. He was very happy for several reasons; mainly because my being so homesick and depressed weighed heavily on him. I was also excited because I had promised to send my mom some money to pay a debt she had. I wanted to help her without imposing on my husband to help – I was the one who had made her that promise. I got all my papers in order and began to work part time; that was completely fine with me.

The day before I was to start at work, I sank deep into a depression. It was pretty bad. I was crying, I was angry. All of the sudden, I did not want to work there. My excitement had turned into bitterness and my husband and I got into a huge fight. He was trying so hard to make me see things in a positive light. I would make friends, he said. I needed to get out of the house. I love children. I will have my own money. But no matter what he said, I was having none of it. He had finally had enough.

"Then don't take the job!"

My husband is even keeled and doesn't really raise his voice but when he does, it is because I have pushed him to his limits and he is at his wit's end. The words that came out of my mouth were not my own; they had not crossed my mind. I replied:

"I have to work there. That is where God wants me to be."

Wait, *what*??? Where did that come from?

The next day, I woke up and immediately started crying. I felt as though my meds had completely stopped working because I was inconsolable. I was confused as well. Why was it that all of the sudden I no longer wanted this job? It was exhausting to say the least. I couldn't get it together. I went to get ready and cried the entire time while I was showering. I found myself doing a lot of that lately. My tears mixed with water from the shower, I couldn't tell where my tears ended and the shower began. The same thought kept going through my mind. *You are supposed to be there. That's where God wants you to go.* The truth is that I had no clue why these thoughts were manifesting. They were not my own.

When I arrived at work, the little children were somewhat skeptical of me. I did not look like them. However, they quickly warmed up to me. My coworkers were amazing women! They were compassionate and showed me around. We went over the schedule and they told me what was to be expected of me. This was Thursday, October 31, 2013. The following Saturday, the school was putting on a sports event for the children and their families and I had to work. I wasn't thrilled about it but it wasn't a choice. I was resisting this job so much but I couldn't tell you why. I enjoyed the work, yet something kept making me feel uneasy. The first day was a success! Before the end of the day, the kids had taken to me and kept hugging me and smiling. I felt great! The void I felt got a bit smaller that day.

On Saturday, Ms. Jackie, the vice principal gave me a ride to the gym where the event would take place. Ms. Jackie was also very nice, but you could tell that she was a little annoyed that her daughter, Misa, was running late. Misa promised to volunteer that day to help out with all the kids. When I met her daughter, I immediately liked her. The day was a riot! I realized that the children were very competitive and wanted to impress their parents. It was a fun day. As we got back to the school, Ms. Jackie turned to her daughter and said:

"Misa, you should invite Ms. Claudia to church tomorrow."

"Ms. Claudia, would you like to go? I think you would enjoy my church, Life House," said Misa.

When I got home, I shared the details of the day's event with Dave. I also told him about the invitation to go to church. I didn't extend it to him because I wasn't sure how he would feel about attending a Christian church, plus my last visit to a church back in the US had left a bitter taste in my mouth and I wasn't sure if I wanted to go myself. He insisted that I go. Part of the reason I didn't want to go was because I still did not know my way around the city and I would have to navigate through multiple train systems to get from Shinagawa to Roppongi. Still, I listened to my husband; he was right–I needed to go out and meet people.

"Here I am! I stand at the door and knock.
If anyone hears My voice and opens the door,
I will come in and eat with him, and he with Me"
Revelation 3:20

My heart was racing because I did not know what to expect. Misa had told me that the service was both in English and Japanese so I would have no problem following, but still, I was very nervous. I felt as nervous as if I was going on a date. *Why?* I called Misa and she didn't answer. I thought to just go back home. However, as I turned the corner and approached the building, I heard lots of laughter and people talking excitedly. Every face I saw had a smile on; it seemed genuine. I had never felt so welcomed at church before. The crowd was not just Japanese. There were people from many parts of the world, but they treated each other like friends, like family. They showed me where to go and I followed the signs that were translated in English and Japanese. Downstairs by the sanctuary, I could not believe how many people were waiting outside to go in as if they were going to their favorite concert or something. When the doors opened, I was escorted to my seat. The lights were dimmed, and the worship team took the stage. As soon as the music started playing, everyone got on their feet and sang along to the lyrics on the screen.

Some people lifted their hands, while others danced to the rhythm of the beat. I watched in amazement. Wow! What a sight to see. I had never witnessed anything like this before. This was different. There was palpable joy in the room.

"You will seek me and find me,
When you seek me with all your heart"
Jeremiah 29:13

During a time of desperation and desolation, when I needed it most, I found Peace. I finally was able to allow joy into my life. The pastor preached a message titled Make a Path for Others and it was as though it had been prepared for me. I felt it in every ounce of my being. Surely, he was speaking to me. I took notes as if I was in school and needed to learn for a test. I wanted to make sure I captured everything he said and in my notes app I jotted down the scriptures he went over and I wrote among other things:

> November 3, 2013 Make a path for others (Day I got saved)
>
> Luke 3:4-6 As it is written in the book of the words of Isaiah the prophet, saying: "the voice of one crying in the wilderness: 'Prepare the way of the Lord; make His paths straight.

Every valley shall be filled and every mountain and hill brought low; the crooked places shall be made straight and the rough ways smooth; and all the flesh shall see the salvation of God"

2 Corinthians 5:17 Therefore, if anyone is in Christ, he is a new creation; old things have passed away; behold, all things have become new. When we are saved by Jesus, we become new; have a new identity. The past no longer matters; God has forgiven me

- Salvation is a new beginning
- Luke 8:16 "No one after lighting a lamp covers it with a vessel, or puts it under a bed, but puts it on a stand, that those who enter may see the light.
- Becoming a Christian is not a part time job, something to do on my spare time; becoming a Christian is ALL the time not when I need it
- Be the light to others
- Let everyone see the new ME and want to follow my light
- My light will now shine forever

Romans 10:13-14 for, "Everyone who calls on the name of the Lord will be saved." 14 How, then, can they call on the one they have not believed in? And how can they believe in the one of whom they have not heard? And how can they hear without someone preaching to them?

- Many people, like myself, think that they are not worthy of having Jesus in their lives; that they are not worthy of being saved but this is the enemy putting binds on us to not let us get closer to God

- Speak to people about God without shoving it down their faces
- Preach without preaching and let my actions do the walking
- There are sooo many souls that need saving but do not know enough about God, about Jesus
- Society is putting a stigma on Christianity and many do not want any of it because of that
- Be kind, be loving, patient, selfless and these things will transform lives because they will want to have what I have!

1 Timothy 2:3-4 This is good, and pleases God our Savior, 4 who wants all people to be saved and to come to a knowledge of the truth.

- God will be pleased with me every time I share my faith with others because God wants everyone to be saved
- How sad it must be for God to have created the earth and everything in it to have us humans destroy not just the earth's environment but each other Make a path for others:
- Be different person: talk, sound and act different. Jesus will change my heart. If I am the same as everyone else, no one will want to follow my path.
- Be willing to speak it out: share about Jesus. Give others the chance to learn about Jesus.
- Never stop: do not give up on people. Do not stop speaking about Jesus. Do not

> stop giving people the chance to learn about Jesus
>
> Romans 8:35 NLT Can anything ever separate us from Christ's love? Does it mean he no longer loves us if we have trouble or calamity, or are persecuted, or hungry, or destitute, or in danger, or threatened with death? "nothing can separate us from the love of Christ"

On November 3, 2013, my eyes were opened to see the Truth. I needed God. As the pastor called the congregation to salvation, I lifted my hand as high as I could and I said yes to Christ. This time was different than the times I said yes before. Something came alive inside me and I wept tears of joy. The eyes of my heart had been enlightened and I understood the hope to which He had called me. As the service ended and the worship team sang their last song "Christ is Enough," I sat there and felt saturated by the Holy Spirit, something I never felt before. During that moment, an Australian woman, Ursula, interrupted me.

"Um, excuse me," she said. "Can I pray for you?"

Nodding my head, I replied.

"Yes. Please."

To be honest, I don't remember all she prayed, but I remember feeling a wave of love and calm inside of me. I saw Misa on my way out and I told her how grateful I was that she invited me to church. She gave me a hug and told me she was so happy for me; she had seen me raise my hand. She invited me back to church next Sunday and told me about the Wednesday service, which took place in a different location. I accepted her invitation and left the church – a new person. I had finally found the hope and peace that I had searched for my whole life.

Chapter Twenty-One

SEEING GOD IN MY LIFE

"I have now seen the One who sees me."
Genesis 16:13

When I got home from church that Sunday, I told my husband all about my encounter with Jesus. I had magically and suddenly fallen in love. It was inexplicable and unexpected. He had rescued me when I needed to be rescued. My whole life I knew there was something greater out there. After all, the evidence was all around me. The creator of all things good was chasing after me. What did I have to lose? Nothing. But I had everything to gain. When I had fallen to my lowest, HE picked me up. Up until then, God had been nothing but a mystical figure to me. Unreachable though I prayed to Him. Now, I understood that prayer was the way to reach Him. He had been there all along, listening to my whispers when I laid in bed as a little girl. HE was there when I felt like I was dying after attempting to take my own life. HE wept with me repeatedly when I cried out in my previous marriage. HE extended his hands when I asked for forgiveness. HE always listened. I couldn't explain why HE allowed my suffering, but I accepted the teaching from it. The character HE built in me and the strength that HE rose from within me. I could not contain my enthusiasm. As I continued to share with him, my husband smiled.

"That's good!"

Such a simple answer, but I knew he meant it. Although, he did not yet share my new understanding of a relationship with God, he could see the joy in my eyes. He knew it had been good for me. When I arrived at work the next day, I still was not over my excitement. I shared my story with everyone who asked me about my weekend. It was a story of love! I had found my first love and I was unashamed about it. Besides, I needed the world to know. Mr. Robert and Mrs. Pauline were overjoyed for me and Ms. Jackie gave me a hug and a smile that lit up the whole school!

Over the next few weeks, God continued to show Himself to me in the workplace. My work schedule was Monday, Tuesday, and Thursday.

I was thrilled to have time off during the week so that I could continue to volunteer at Hands on Tokyo, a non-profit organization. Prior to getting my new job, I had enjoyed volunteering and cherished every moment I spent with the elderly and children with special needs. However, on my first Wednesday off, I was scheduled to volunteer but I decided not to go. I was wrestling with my thoughts because I missed my family and as much as I wanted to enjoy my new surroundings, I couldn't, so I stayed in bed most of the day. When I arrived at work the next Thursday, I was talking to one of my coworkers when I learned that they only pay once a month, and that I would have to wait two months before my first paycheck. *Great!* I thought to myself, that would be my excuse to quit. Hearing that news, I asked Mr. Robert and Mrs. Pauline if I could have a word with them before the end of the day. They agreed and suggested we talk while the children napped.

During nap time, I sat down with my new bosses and was firmly set on quitting. I told them how grateful I was that they gave me this opportunity; but it was a mistake. I explained that I had recently learned of the monthly pay—and I would have to wait two months to receive my first paycheck. I mentioned the train fare was quite expensive commuting from Shinagawa. I gave them excuse after excuse. Mrs. Pauline said they would make an exception and I would get paid at the end of my first month. Still making excuses, I told them that wouldn't work. My mother was expecting me to send her money that I had earned the previous weeks.

"How much?" They asked.

I gave them an amount then Mr. Robert stepped away. When he returned, he handed me a check. It was for the amount I had given them. I started to cry. He indicated that it was not a loan, nor would it be deducted from my paycheck. When I refused, he replied.

"You cannot take away our blessing." He continued: "When we bless others, God blesses us in return."

He also told me that they would be paying for my commute. It seemed like nothing I said to these two people would work. At that very instant I had a mental conversation with God. The God I had just said yes to. The God I had recently fallen in love with. This is when I said a silent prayer in my head: *Okay God, if you want me to stay here, then Mr. Robert has to tell me that I am here because YOU want me to be here.* No sooner did I finish this brief mental conversation than Mr. Robert looked sternly at me and said these words that I will never forget:

"You think you are here because of your husband? You are not. You are here because God wants you to be here."

I wept when I heard these words and asked them to forgive me for making so many excuses to push them away. I shared my silent prayer with them and how they had unknowingly answered my prayer. God had listened. More importantly, Mr. Robert's words had shown me God's greater purpose for my trip to Japan. To reveal Himself to me and to my husband.

When I got home, I shared all that had transpired with Dave and we both were astounded that such things could be happening. That is how God works. I started using my commute to read scripture and learn about God's nature and characters. This beautiful, invisible but very real God. Unless you are in a relationship with Jesus, you can't understand how I felt. It's a feeling that cannot be explained merely with words. It was a sudden joy! For the first time in my entire life, I felt an inexplicable love. Inexplicable, because I wasn't worthy of such love. A love that in an instant started to change me. I went to church on Wednesday night and once more, I couldn't wait to tell my husband all about it. The pastor preached a good word titled "I am a Seed." My fingers were trying very hard to keep up with the word that was being taught. I realized that despite my messed-up upbringing, how I did so many things that I regretted, I was still a good seed because I had been living under a veil and that veil was being torn apart! I secretly yearned for my husband to start coming to church with me on Sunday, but I didn't want to push so I didn't ask.

Chapter Twenty-Two

A NEW ME

"Delight yourself in the Lord,
And He will give you the desires of your heart."
Psalm 37:4

The next few months were a time of constant prayer and tears. I was shedding my old skin and allowing God to chisel off my shame, my guilt. For decades, I had lived with such regret. My thoughts went all the way back to my grandparents. I had been disobedient and inconsiderate toward these two gray-haired human beings. I had not even attended my grandpa's funeral when he died at 103 years old. That one still stings! They had given the last of their old age strength to caring for my sisters and I. I owe them so much; I took them for granted and I carried the guilt of how I had treated them my entire life. Sitting at my kitchen table I prayed the following: "God, please forgive me for all the people I hurt growing up. Forgive me for the headaches I caused my grandparents as a child. Forgive me Lord for disrespecting my grandpa, the only man who truly loved me when I was a child."

In the middle of that prayer, I also found forgiveness for myself. It didn't take away the sting of missing them, but I no longer had to carry the guilt of my past actions. I would give anything for the chance of one last hug. If I close my eyes and go back to the time when I was just a child, I can feel my grandpa's hand on mine. Those same hands that worked so hard until he could not any longer. I could still smell the scent of his cigar and his pipe. I could still hear him so close to me asking me for a little coffee or aguapanela to drink. Oh, how I miss my grandpa. I imagined this is what loving an earthly father felt like. After all, he was that for me.

Still sitting at my kitchen table, crying, I continued to ask God to forgive me.

"God, forgive me for being disobedient."

I wept as I spoke those words. I wept over the two lives that were cut short because of my actions. For years I tormented myself thinking about my unborn children. Every year since, I would go over the approximate age of each child. I would calculate "this child would be 'x' years old and this one 'y' years old." I had to let go of the guilt.

"Lord, forgive me for cutting those lives short."

I don't know that I will reunite with them when I come face to face with my Jesus but I like to think that I will see all those who have gone before me. I like to think that before the unsaved take their last breath, Jesus makes one last attempt to save their souls. Isn't that why He died on the cross?

My next prayer that day was for the mom and her son that I had robbed.

"God, please forgive me for having been part of the assault on that woman and her son. Forgive me for not standing up and saying no when it felt so wrong. Forgive my weaknesses. God, I pray that both the woman and her son forgive me also."

As I thought of my horrible actions, almost unable to even pray because praying meant using my voice to say aloud and acknowledge once more what a disaster my life had been. The images of those two strangers haunted me and I deserved it.

My final prayer that day was for my sins committed during my first marriage.

"God, please forgive me for my indiscretions and infidelity in my previous marriage. Hugo did not deserve that. Forgive me for cheating all those years and using excuse after excuse, Lord. There is no excuse Father for my actions. Forgive all my sexual immoralities."

Praying and asking for forgiveness allowed me to see His goodness surface. His grace covered me like a blanket swaddling an infant! I felt forgiven. I had been redeemed of my past.

Similar to how Jesus walked and dined with those who didn't know His love, He still died for them. Perhaps I was as unlovable as Judas or the murderous thief at the cross, yet the thief found redemption at the cross. Perhaps I was no different than the woman in John 8 who was caught searching for love in the wrong places. Similar to Pharaoh who had instructed all children be slaughtered incited by fear of losing his kingdom; I had made a choice out of fear and consented to end the lives of two of my own children.

Before I gave my life back to Jesus, I did not believe it was possible to be forgiven. I refused to believe that all you needed was to ask for forgiveness and repent. How could you commit such heinous acts and ask to be forgiven and heaven will open for you? There was no way it was that simple. But it is. God sees our hearts. He weeps with us. He catches our tears. He laughs when we laugh and hurts when we hurt. He hurts when we go against His will – for HIS will is to bless and show His favor. And though He is in control, He will never force Himself on us. In my case, He had allowed me to go through the fire until I surrendered.

He was there every single step of the way. He wept with me when my father sexually abused me, when his wife's brother did the same. When my other family member did the same. Although I wanted them to hurt as much as they hurt me and hurt badly. But God found me!

Holding on to all of that hurt was crippling my capacity to know His love. When I made my heart available, I was able to experience forgiveness–I understood that God wants to redeem everyone; even those who hurt me. Understanding His love allowed me to forgive knowing that forgiveness is not about establishing relationships but letting go. Everything they did to me bears consequences – but it's up to God to deal with the legacy of my birth father's brokenness.

Even still, Father God always had a plan for me despite my awful past – He will complete His work in me – that's His promise. He collected each of my tears and exchanged it for His goodness. God had been there in the sterile room as I aborted His children. He cried with me as He wiped my tears of uncertainty. God had been there when I assaulted that woman and her son. He wiped my tears of brokenness. God was there when I committed adultery. He wiped my tears of betrayal. God wiped my tears every single time. Each tear represented heaviness and bore consequences. I made choices and so did those that hurt me. Although, God did not cause it – HE was there with me helping me heal and waiting on me. I was never alone.

Saturday, after spending the entire day out exploring, I told my husband that I was going to church the next day. He could tell how excited I was and he told me that he wanted to go with me. I was exhilarated! He wanted to go to support me, but he was also curious about what was causing the change he saw in me and ever since that day, my husband and I started to put Jesus in our marriage.

The next day on our way home, I was still on a high from church and excited to hear Dave's impression. I was elated to hear that he had enjoyed it and wanted to attend with me again. That same Sunday, a new friend invited me to attend a LifeGroup and though it was yet another first for me, I was happy to go. There I met a young woman whose love for God exuded through her pores. She could have been a billboard of a Christian woman! We became quick friends. She is from Arizona but had been living in Japan for a while. There she met the man of her life and they soon married and now were parents to a little Japanese American boy. Sarah introduced me to her LifeGroup friends who took the time to teach me about the God of scripture.

"Love the Lord your God with all your heart,
all your soul, all your mind, and all your strength"
Mark 12:30

I remember how crazy in love I was for Christ. It was like I couldn't get enough of Him. I needed more of Him. I started to listen to worship music on my way to and from work as I read the Bible and took notes. And though this newfound love for God was beautiful, it was also very confusing. I kept being told that I needed to put God first in my life. To be honest, that was a scary thought. I was reading scripture daily and I was falling hard for God but put Him first? *How?* My daughters were first in my life. I did not know what to do and the next day, while getting ready for work, I began to cry in the shower. *God, how can I put you first?* My daughters come first in my life. I spent over a decade in a toxic marriage for my girls because I put them first and now, I was expected to put them second? No way! I had to break up with God but I didn't know how. When I got to work, Mr. Robert must have sensed my troubled spirit because he asked me how I was doing? Mr. Robert enjoyed teaching me about scripture and never got annoyed when I asked him questions. This time, instead of a cheerful answer, I told him about my dilemma.

"Mr. Robert," I said with tears streaming down my face, "How can I put Jesus first? I don't know how to do that!"

With compassion, Mr. Robert read a few bible verses for me. Through these verses I received clarity about His wonderful love. I could cast my cares to Him. If I put Him first, he would provide for me. He who created my daughters, could do more for them than I ever could! Everything was created by Him for Him. Mr. Robert told me that if I put God first, He would always take care of my daughters. His explanation made so much sense and since that day,

God has been number one in my life. Reading His Word revealed His love for me. I began to journal on His Word and on November 20th, I emailed my twin sister asking her if we could walk this Christian walk together. I explained my new view on God and shared the notes that I took the previous Sunday. I just felt a need to tell anyone who could hear me about Jesus. Everyone I knew needed what I had discovered, a Love that was selfless, pure, kind, forgiving. A Love that would die for me again and again. I looked up to my twin sister because for years she had been following Christ, she was in a relationship with God. I also wanted to hear my mom's input because she loved God. This was evident from early on when she moved in with us, when she had been diagnosed with lymphoma. My mom would spend hours in the Word. My new relationship with God was also affecting my other relationships in a good way. I was feeling alive! Jesus came into my life not so that I would follow a set of rules but so that I could come alive through Him. I had written my twin sister:

"Christians must live the Word of God but it doesn't mean that we have to live a perfect life, it doesn't mean that we can't get mad, sad or be upset when we hurt, it just means that when we are mad, upset, or even sad, we understand that it will just be temporary. That whatever it is that we are feeling, will not be permanent, for Jesus already died to take our sorrows away."

In only 17 days since I opened my heart to Jesus, I already started to understand His essence little by little much like a child who starts to recognize her mother's scent. God was speaking to me and I was listening!

"He said to her, 'Daughter, your faith has healed you.
Go in peace and be freed from your suffering'"
Mark 5:34

Although mentally and spiritually I was in a better place, physically I was not. I was having back problems for some time and it was only getting worse. While standing on my train ride to and from work, I would feel my back pop and spasm. Feeling the pain radiate down my leg I became afraid. There were days I could do nothing but lay down in bed because of the pain. Even a friend that worked as a Physicians Assistant for an orthopedic surgeon suggested I get checked out. On Sunday at church, during our LifeGroup, we talked about pain and healing. I shared a bit of the pain I was experiencing and Sarah mentioned that Pastor Rod was preaching on healing. She encouraged me and suggested that should he make an altar call, I should go get prayed over. She said God was the only one who could heal me. Right after the LifeGroup ended, I met up with my husband (yes, he was now attending a men's small group too) and we went together into the service. The title of Pastor Rod's message was "The Healing Power of Jesus." Pastor Rod shared the story about the woman with the issue of blood found in Mark 5. If Jesus healed her, surely, He could heal me too. I was ready to let go of my pain. Carrying that pain was so draining for me. The Word was timely and precise. It was just for me. God was speaking to me by using the man on stage.

I understood that it may not happen overnight and if I didn't give up, God would heal me. Jesus could heal me emotionally, and restore my hope and vision. I wrote down God's promise and how all things are possible for Him and that He would not forsake me. I heard for the first time to not be shy nor modest but to take what is mine, the promise of God to heal my life. All I needed to do was ask and Jesus could heal my body, mind, vision, and desires. What a service! I knew one thing for sure, if they made an altar call for healing, I was walking forward. Just as the service was coming to an end and with the worship team already on stage, I was praising and crying. My back starting popping and cracking and the pain was debilitating. I wanted to sit down but the service was almost over and I decided to tough it out. I was crying out for God to please heal me. At that moment, I didn't care about my emotional pain. I was pleading with God to heal my back; to take that physical pain away. Finally, the altar-call for healing and I was one of the first ones to walk up. I closed my eyes and in faith I prayed that God would heal me. I envisioned the woman with the issue of blood, who knew that if she could only touch the hem of Jesus' garment she would be healed, and her bleeding would stop. I pictured myself like that woman; I didn't really know Jesus, but He sure knew me. I felt and heard people praying over me. Most of the prayers I did not understand at all because they were praying in Japanese but I sensed they were praying for me among many other people.

Before leaving church that day, Sarah explained the meaning of baptism. I understood it to be like kissing my old life away and welcoming a new life. Being set free from my past and committing myself to trying to live a life of doing good. She reminded me to have a frank conversation with the Lord and repent. Repentance brings freedom. I did not want to waste any more time. Imagine, God took me across the world so I could surrender to Him! How beautiful was that? He chased me for so long; I didn't heed His calling nor His knocking. Now that I had decided to open my heart to Him, I wanted it all. I could not wait to get baptized! The night before my baptism, I didn't sleep much. In fact, most nights that week, I was plagued by nightmares. I couldn't find rest.

Baptism was on the following Saturday at a different location. That morning, I was nervous yet eager to make this public declaration of my love for God. Saying yes seemed like getting engaged, it was an intimate moment between the Lord and I; getting baptized was like a wedding in front of new friends and my new family. Misa would be there cheering me on and I was overjoyed that she would witness my baptism. After all, if it hadn't been for that invitation to church, I would still be a lost sheep. Sarah would also be there and that meant the world to me. Not only was Sarah my small group leader and one of the pastors' wives but in the short time I'd known her, she had opened her home to us and become a close friend. We celebrated Thanksgiving together. Sarah knew the pain of missing my family during the holiday, so she insisted my husband and I share with them and a few other friends. As we were about to leave our tiny apartment, it hit me, it was my first revelation. I turned to my husband and asked him a question that was more like a statement:

"You know what? Tomorrow will be one week since I last experienced back pain!"

I had not taken any pain meds since the previous Sunday when I went forward for healing. I bent my back and tried motions that had caused me pain before. I was dumbfounded.

"No pain at all!"

I told him that my back hadn't popped and the pain radiating down my leg was completely gone. I did a little dance and jumped for joy. This was my own miracle! I turned to my husband completely elated.

"Honey, I am healed. Jesus healed my back."

It was a revelation and realization. I experienced first-hand God's healing miracle! Similar to my mom who was healed from cancer; I now believed that three doctors hadn't made the same mistake. God healed her. Just like He healed me now. It was easier to disbelieve the miracle when I was spiritually blind. Oh, how foolish of me. I used to think that it took great effort and time to have faith to believe in miracles. But it is really as simple as just believing. Now, faith is all I have, and it is the easiest part of my new journey. Faith is believing and hoping, but a hope that reassures me that my prayers will not fall on deaf ears because God cares about every detail of my life.

I was almost late to my own baptism because we missed our train stop. Sarah had warned me that I would likely hit obstacles before my baptism. She advised me to pray. Since she knew my story – she said not to be surprised if I had nightmares. Supposedly, these are a common occurrence leading up to baptism. I must confess that on my way to being baptized, I was angry. The irony! My anger perhaps a result of anxieties that I could miss it. One of my pet peeves is tardiness but my husband kept reassuring me that we would make it. He's good at making me feel better.

When we finally arrived, the place was packed. There was so much going on; a lot of commotion. I felt very jittery but when it was my turn, the jitters turned to rejoicing. I am not going to lie, I thought that when I came up from being submerged in the water, I would all of the sudden feel different, like I would physically feel the Holy Spirit. Perhaps it was all those visions of Jesus being baptized and the Holy Spirit descending on Him that had me thinking that everyone's experience was the same. What I felt was cold and couldn't wait to change my clothing. I was drenched. It was chilly outside with temperature in the mid-fifties. Somehow watching all the people, mostly young folks, warmed me up inside.

That afternoon after baptism, my husband and I celebrated this historical event in my life with dinner. That day, I made a conscious decision to portray my love for God and joy to be walking with Him. Unlike the baptism when I was a little girl, I had no say in the matter, this time it was my declaration of love and I wanted the whole world to know! It was not about religion but relationship. I was on fire for God and could not get enough of Him.

"Delight yourself in the Lord,
And He will give you the desires of your heart"
Psalm 37:4

The holidays were approaching and we missed our children and family so much! We felt blessed to have celebrated Thanksgiving with friends, but Christmas was coming along with an overwhelming feeling of sadness knowing we would not be home for the holidays. Christmas in Japan would be unlike anything we had experienced. Although, we had more friends than ever, both from church and not, and we were finally having a great time, the thought of not seeing the family for Christmas was unbearable. Except that instead of crying and feeling sorry for myself, my cries were accompanied with prayers. My husband and I began praying that we would be able to go home for the holidays to see our family at the company's expense! We knew it was a far-fetched prayer, but we still prayed. Since my husband attended church with me, we began praying together. It was beautiful to hear him pray. Soon after, my husband called one afternoon to tell me that the company would pay for our trip home for the holidays! I could not believe what I'd just heard! This was a specific answer to our prayers! That same evening, we decided to surprise the family as we purchased our tickets to go home.

On Christmas Eve 2013, we were on our way home to the U.S. As I sat on the plane, I opened up my notes app and wrote a short prayer. I put my life and everyone's on the plane in God's hands. I thanked and praised Him for making this trip possible. It was by His grace and not because we had earned it. We left Japan on Christmas Eve, luckily as we crossed the International Date Line, we arrived on U.S. soil early Christmas Eve. It was perfect since Christmas Eve is our big celebration. Our first stop was my in-laws' home. They were pleasantly surprised and my mother-in-law's laughter filled the room. As now a blended family, we made a few stops to see my step kids. Then to see my girls. I called my girls from the car and we FaceTime'd the entire ride. They were clueless that we were not in Japan. I don't know how they missed the signs especially the time difference. We were still on the phone when we got to the house and I rang the bell. I said:

"Someone is at the door, open it."

Then I heard my little one crying overtaken by emotion when she became aware that we were on the other side of the door! She was in utter disbelief. Once inside the house,

I couldn't stop hugging them and kissing them. I didn't want to let them go.

We received the same reaction from everyone else. They could not believe we were there! It was beautiful! We spent Christmas Eve at my twin sister's home with the extended family and I continuously kept thanking God for making it happen. A few days later, while I was visiting my daughters, I began to talk to them about my new walk with Christ. I had a deep longing for them to be saved. Besides, I needed to share what I finally understood about Him and His love for us. I said: "Hey, you know how I'd always talked to you about God? Like when we said grace before dinner? I would say God this and God that."

One of them sheepishly replied,

"Yes."

The word hung awkwardly in the air waiting for me to continue. "Well, I've talked to you about God but I never talked to you about Jesus." Let me tell you about Jesus: He is the Way, the Truth and the Life and He says that no one can go to the Father except through Him."

And I explained the best way I could what that meant. My Christian walk had just started. I was still a baby in the faith, but I tried to describe the new me and how saying yes to Jesus had changed my life. We made plans to attend church once we came back for good, which would be in just a couple more months. Leaving for the second time was not easier than the first time. In fact, I was saddened because I wanted to stay with them and my sister. A couple more months would go fast.

"You keep him in perfect peace whose mind is stayed on you, because he trusts in you"
Isaiah 26:3

Life was good! My new feeling of joy in Jesus was changing my outlook in life and I started to have faith. The faith scripture talks about became my reality. Faith that gave me hope for the things not yet seen was what I needed as I continued pressing through depression. But as I started to turn my focus to Him, I felt better. My new daily routine included reading scripture every morning after my husband left to work. I watched online services from Lakewood Church or Church of the Highlands and continued to take notes. In the evening, after dinner, while my husband watched a little TV, I continued to journal. In my notebook, I would start with just the date. After reading scripture and allowing the Word to seep in, I would pick the verse that spoke to my heart and I would write what my spirit heard and closed it with a prayer. Once I had completed those steps, I'd give it a title to make it easier to recall where I was in my walk if I ever went back to read it. This new practice showed me how faithful God had been over the years. Not knowing enough back then, I had found God in the stars at night. As I journaled, I learned about my new identity. I reflected on loving others similar to how Jesus loves me; being like God's mirror. Once my focus turned to His love and faithfulness from one day to the next, I no longer needed my meds for depression. It wasn't that suddenly my sadness and pain went away but I was consumed by Him and I felt like I could face just about anything! I started to understand that I was no longer fighting my battles alone. I was on top of the world. The daughter of the King. Above and not beneath! I was on my way toward my new identity.

I thought that I would be on antidepressants my whole life. It was such a foreign feeling of euphoria. I am thankful that God gave doctors the gift for healing through medicine. I benefited from medication and therapy and was never ashamed by it. I kept the rest of my meds by the bed in case I needed them. But I didn't. HE reminded me through HIS word that it was ok to feel sad, it was normal to be angry as well. The WORD helped me press through the shame and guilt of my past behaviors. It was a challenge – I even had several tough conversations with Jesus about my feelings.

Although I didn't hear him speak back, I felt him – and that was more than enough.

I once heard someone say: "If you are depressed, you are living in the past. If you are anxious, you are living in the future. If you are at peace, you are living in the present." That statement reminded me of living in God's presence. The more I was getting to know Him, the more I was blessed. I don't know how to explain it but my prayers were being answered. The size of my prayer didn't matter; He was answering them.

Around this time, one day after work, my husband told me that his work assignment would be extended. I had mixed emotions about this. I was enjoying my time in Tokyo and the people we met were incredible. Life seemed simpler; people took pleasure in smaller things like getting a group together to play Frisbee or go for a picnic at the park. Our weekends were full of activities – volunteering, visiting new sites, spending time with friends. Of course, we missed our children immensely; each day I wished to hug my daughters and my sister. However, I was finally in a good place mentally and wanted to stay. I was able to experience ways that God continuously blessed us. Our choices were: stay in Japan seven more months, go to Singapore, or come back to the states to look for a new job. It would be hard telling the kids. But the obvious choice was to stay. I honestly wasn't ready to come back home. Perhaps I was terrified that I wasn't ready to walk alone. I didn't know of any church in New York. My only experiences had been the churches I attended with my sister and mom. They were not what I experienced in Japan – they seemed super judgmental. I felt in my heart that I needed to find a church of my own before I went home. I didn't want to go back to my old life nor walk away. During my quick visit at Christmas, I visited a church – but it was not the church I would call home. I still had so many questions about God, the Trinity, how it all worked. I would constantly reach out to Sarah asking her for clarity on scripture; if we went home, who would help me grow? Who would I reach out to for answers? Sarah would be on the other side of the world with 13 hours' time difference, who would have time to wait for an answer? Staying for another six months seemed like the right thing to do.

As much as I loved my job and adored the little kids, I was ready to quit. There was nothing in particular that I didn't like. I would miss the children very much. My bosses favored me – it even felt awkward around my colleagues. With an already great work ethic, now as a Christian, I went the extra mile, for now I understood the scripture and how it says work for men as onto the Lord. And it didn't matter what my chore was, I did it to the best of my abilities with love in my heart. If it was my turn to clean the bathroom, I wiped the toilet and sink squeaky clean. I polished the tables and every chair until every little fingerprint was erased and spotless. I truly loved my time at the pre-school and will forever be grateful to Mr. Robert and Mrs. Pauline for giving me the chance to work for them. God used these two people to introduce me to Him. It was three days after I started working at the school that I met Misa. She invited me to church and the very next day I came face to face with my savior. The lengths to which God will go to chase after us!

I was genuinely sad when I thought of not being around the students anymore but I had become friends with one of my students' mom and I knew we would continue our friendship beyond the school. Thank God for Google, which we used to communicate! We were determined to stay in touch.

I gave my boss a month's notice so they would have ample time to find my replacement. On my last day of work, Mrs. Pauline told me that I was the first person from "America" they hired. Americans don't have the best "reputation" of work ethic. She said that when we met, she wasn't sure about me at first but as we engaged in conversation, she felt something in her spirit and knew they were supposed to offer me the job. God works all things for good.

My fortieth birthday was approaching and I had never spent a birthday away from my family. I started praying for God to make a way for us to be back home in time to celebrate. God answered that prayer also and we bought our plane tickets and started counting the days!

My husband and my sister's boyfriend started to plan a "surprise birthday party" for my twin and I. In case you forgot, I do not like surprises at all. In fact, the only time that I wanted to be surprised was when I was pregnant with my girls. Anyway, somehow, I found out about the surprise party they were devising, and I rolled up my sleeves to help. I wanted to make sure that my sister had an amazing birthday. She deserved to be celebrated with all the bells and whistles. We enlisted the girls help too and they also got to work.

The party did not disappoint. We walked inside and my sister covered her face with both hands when she saw all the guests waiting to give her a hug. What a great memory! The party was better than planned. The girls did a phenomenal job decorating and had carefully chosen the small colorful vases and taken care of all the details; I was a proud mom. The DJ had us dancing the entire time. The only time we sat down was to eat and when a musician we hired started to play his acoustic guitar, my sister and her boyfriend found themselves on the dance floor dancing alone. Before we knew it, her boyfriend was down on one knee proposing to her. What a privilege to have been part of such an occasion.

We spent the last three weeks of our trip with the family treasuring every moment with them because I knew I wouldn't see them again for another four months.

"In my distress I prayed to the Lord,
And the Lord answered me and set me free"
Psalm 118:5

My relationship with Jesus was changing my life for the better one battle at a time and next up was porn. I fought my addiction to porn.I always felt dirty afterwards.

I despised it. I always hated it! I didn't know how to break such addiction.

It was my secret; the only thing I kept secret from my husband. And one afternoon while he was at work, I gave in to my flesh and I turned my eyes toward the screen and defiled my spirit. The guilt consumed me—I wanted to die and not disappoint my heavenly Father. I got on my knees and opened my arms in surrender. "God, please forgive me and cleanse me." I could not hide from my shame. I found myself in a fetal position crying. I prayed so hard that afternoon. I prayed for God to break the chains of addiction. "Free me, oh Lord." I said. "Remove my shackles and free me from the hand of addiction" I said with tears in my eyes.

Instantaneously the chain of addiction broke off and that was the last time I ever felt compelled to watch pornography. His grace became bigger than my desires. I choose grace over guilt! Sin only leads to guilt and love leads to His grace.

Little by little I learned that addiction was no longer part of my identity. Healing had finally begun! The problem with addiction is that it is not ever completely gone; you have to be vigilant to not fall back into it. The devil will have you doubt your restoration, and that it's a continuous cycle of sin. That was farthest from the truth for me!! Since that momentous afternoon in a tiny room in Japan, I have been set free from the addiction of pornography. Addiction is broken by the renewing of the mind. It is through repentance that one can change. I was on my knees crying out to God asking for forgiveness. I was sincere in my repentance and believed that God could remove the feeling of filth. HE surely did.

"Search me, O God, and know my heart;
Try me, and know my anxieties;
And see if there is any wicked way in me,
And lead me in the way everlasting"
Psalm 139:23

However, my new life in Christ came with some challenges. The biggest was accepting my new creation in Christ. I still had such anger inside of me and any tiny spark would ignite a fire. Anger would take the best of me and turn me into my worst self. I wanted to come home and I didn't know how to deal with this feeling and I would end up lashing out at my husband who always took my aggression in stride and didn't fight back. One day, after a HUGE blow out and saying many regretful things, I penned a letter to God expressing my remorse:

"June 2, 2014

Dear God,
Today, I've been bad.
God, I am turning to you. Are you listening? Can you see the pain in my heart?
God, can you make my spirit stronger than my heart? than my flesh? Can you remove my feelings and pour your love in me instead?
God, are you even listening? can you see my pain? Did you leave me, God?
because right now I am not feeling very loved. Right now my anger overtakes me and makes me say things that are bad, things that I know I will regret.
I thought that this wouldn't happen. I thought that I would always feel you inside and that your love would change me but God, I don't feel that right now.
Right now, I feel different, I feel scared, angry, sad and disappointed. I feel like I am drowning!! WHY???? why do I feel like you have left me? Or have I been the one to walk away?
God, please forgive me. SAVE ME!! I am drowning! I need you Lord, I need you.

> Wipe my tears, clean my heart. Please wrap your goodness around me please. Make me sleep and forget who I am. God, have I not changed at all???
> Why do I feel like the enemy is taking hold of me??? why God, You
> Promise [sic] You would not let that happen but yet I feel like I can't even
> breathe. I feel like I am suffocating, like I cannot even breathe.
> I feel like I am alone, left alone with my anger and hurtful words. God, can you hear what I am saying?
> Can you see my pain?
> God, are you listening? God, can you see me? Did you decide that I am nothing?
> Please don't abandon me, Lord. Can you see that I need You?
>
> I AM CALLING YOU LORD!!! COME, PLEASE TAKE ME! PLEASE CHANGE ME. CHANGE MY HEART. CLEAN IT GOD. "

I really did feel like I was drowning inside. I felt torn. I wanted to come home in the worst way possible yet I kept on praying for God not to allow me to return home if I wasn't ready. "Lord, please help me find a church in New York and only then I will go back. Lord, I am not ready to be on my own. Please help."

I then called my husband and asked for forgiveness.

"You did not deserve to be treated that way. Who am I to talk to you like that?"

My groom is the true definition of 1 Corinthians 13:4-7. Never has he thrown in my face my mistakes nor held anything against me. This time he also remained steadfast. Instead, he told me that he understood my frustration and that he would not blame me if I flew home earlier. He said he preferred I stay with him until he completed the last few months of his assignment, but he would not hold me back. He also told me that he would prefer I wait until I found a church I could call home. Yet, even though he had accepted my apology, my shame at my outburst did not subside. I cried some more and spent the rest of the day in bed.

The next day, I felt an urge to write again. However, this time I wrote not my own thoughts but what I heard in my spirit.

"June 3, 2014

Dear child,
No, my child, you are never bad. Since you reached out to me and let me grabbed your hand, you have not an ounce of bad in you. See, you don't understand but sometimes you feel alone but you can't be because I am all around you. You know that suffocating feeling, that feeling that you couldn't breathe? That is because my arms were all around you. I was hugging you so tight that I was taking your breath away.

That moment when you thought that you were all cried out of tears, no my daughter you hadn't ran out of tears, I was wiping them away before they roll [sic] down your face.

You asked me to help make you sleep so that you could forget who you are but I couldn't do that at that moment because to forget who you are is to forget what I have done in your life and how far you have come.

My daughter, my child, don't ever be afraid that I would leave you or let you walk away; that's impossible because you have been imprinted with me! See, I love you so much that I sometimes have to let you fall. And one more thing, when you were sad, so was I because I am your Father and it hurts me to see my daughter hurt. Isn't this what happens to you when your kids hurt? Don't you feel their pain? I'm no different, in fact I hurt more. I heard you crying, I heard your pleads [sic]. I heard you calling me and waiting for me. But my child, in your despair would you have listened to me?

Don't forget that I love you, don't think you can walk away because my child, I'm all around you and I am here to stay!

Love~ your father, God"

Chapter Twenty-Three

FINAL REMARKS

It has been quite the walk! Since leaving Japan, I have found an amazing church to call my home. Over the years, God has continued to work on my life and heal me from my hurt and my sin. He's also given me amazing opportunities to serve others and share His love. I still want to pinch myself sometimes.

I have been redeemed by our Creator. I used to see myself as insignificant, not worthy of much. That was a banner that I had placed on myself: unworthy. Unworthy of love and because of that, I spent the majority of my life searching for love in the wrong places or not caring enough to ask for the love that I deserved. Jesus changed all that in an instant. He reminded me that He places value in me. I am worthy because He lives in me. The devil would have us think that we are nothing, incapable of much. The enemy turns our weaknesses into our struggles and uses our fears as weapons against us and because we don't know any better, we believe his lies. That is until we listen to the voice of the Father. Jesus is the Way, the Truth and the Life. We have to believe that we don't have to work to earn God's love but what we fail to see is that His love is freely given to anyone who wants it. His Son carried the cross because He loves us that much. You may not know Jesus but Jesus knows you. He is right there as close as your breath; just like He had been there all along with me. You may not yet be in Him but He is already in you. My earthly father had me thinking that I was damaged goods, but God said I AM good and His goodness will never run out. I still have my struggles and I believe that as a human being, I always will but the years of abuse no longer define me. I am defined by what the Word of God says. I have no ill feeling toward anyone who did me wrong; how could I? I did so many people wrong. I did God wrong and yet He went after me and forgave me and still does. I am not perfect, and I thank God for that. Achieving perfection is a fool's belief that they don't need Jesus in their lives. God has always been faithful to me and caught every tear I cried. He held me when I needed to be held as a child. He loved me when others didn't. He has cared for me.

> *"If you declare with your mouth, "Jesus is Lord,"*
> *and believe in your heart that God raised Him*
> *from the dead, you will be saved."*
> *Romans 10:9*

I did so many things that I am not proud of. Things probably horrified you when you read them. That's okay. It is my story of redemption and a story of hope for those who need HIM.

If you are going through life alone, you need a savior, and His name is Jesus. What do you have to lose? Look at me and see all I've gained. I will spend my eternity in the company of God, in heaven. Taking walks with Jesus and listening to the counsel of the Holy Spirit. That alone was worth dying to my old self. Jesus doesn't love me more than He loves YOU. He loves you the same because He also died for you even though YOU also did not deserve it and guess what? I believe in my heart that He would die for us again and again all so that we can be in relationship with Him. God will not change you but it is YOUR love for Him that will. God loves you right there where you are and is waiting on you to come to Him. What are you waiting for?

Ingram Content Group UK Ltd.
Milton Keynes UK
UKHW020626260523
422394UK00013B/311